ENCHANTED

TITANIA'S BOOK OF WHITE MAGIC

ENCHANTED

TITANIA'S BOOK OF WHITE MAGIC

TITANIA HARDIE

PHOTOGRAPHS BY SARA MORRIS

WILLIAM MORROW & COMPANY, INC. · NEW YORK

My previous book, TITANIA'S ORAQLE, was dedicated to the wonderful women in my life.

This volume is for the wonderful men: Peter Charell, my father, who gave me a warm Italian heart, and Shakespeare;

John Flynn, Austin Pritchard Levy, and Andrew Huntley, who introduced me to the extraordinary realm of the

metaphysical when I was 17 or 18; Mozart, who daily brings the music of the spheres to my ears;

Samuel Taylor Coleridge, my "best friend"; Philip Whelan, Lawrence Ewing, Orlando Murrin, Paul Ross, and Richard Madeley,

all inspirationally accomplished and creative at their work; Dr. Leslie Hoose and Hamish Johnson, at the Open University,

who feed my soul and mind with a perpetual feast and try to keep me somewhat rational (well, they try!);

and the Losey men—Joe, Gavrik, Luke, Joshua, and Marek, who all dare(d) to be very different.

GREAT THINGS ARE DONE WHEN MEN AND MOUNTAINS MEET;
THIS IS NOT DONE BY JOSTLING IN THE STREET.
William Blake

Also by Titania Hardie
HOCUS POCUS Titania's Book of Spells
BEWITCHED Titania's Book of Love Spells
TITANIA'S ORAQLE A Unique Way to Predict Your Future
Titania's Wishing Spells LOVE
Titania's Wishing Spells HAPPINESS

Text copyright © 1999 by Titania Hardie
Photography © 1999 Sara Morris
Layout and design copyright © 1999 Quadrille Publishing Ltd
First published in 1999 by Quadrille Publishing Limited,
Alhambra House, 27–31 Charing Cross Road, London WC2H 0LS

Library of Congress Cataloging-in-Publication Data available upon request.

ISBN 0-688-17366-7

Printed in Hong Kong
First Edition
1 2 3 4 5 6 7 8 9 10
BOOK DESIGN by johnson banks
www.williammorrow.com

INTRODUCING WHITE MAGIC: You are invited to a witches' tea party. My own favorite brew is Earl Grey, but do please join me with a cup of whatever you fancy. Tie a purple ribbon around your cup—you will understand why within a few pages!

As we make the journey through this book—and thereby through the philosophy and observance of WICCA custom—it is important to understand two basic truths. There is no room in the true witch's thoughts for arrogance toward others' religious beliefs, for all approaches to contemplating the divine, creative force are considered valid and honorable; no one should believe that their own approach is the only justified belief system. Then, too, it is vital to understand that if we as individuals have a right to happiness here on earth, now—as indeed does everyone else—we cannot contravene this spiritual truth by seeking our own pleasure and wishes at the cost of anyone else's. This demands that no individual be on the receiving end of our angry spells, or that we direct "bad feeling" to others—no matter how great we may feel the provocation to be. The only way in which the true Wicca creed allows for "revenge" over others is by our surpassing those who have done or wished us harm. In other words, think not of getting even, but rather of leaving petty-minded people far behind by attracting a much stronger and beneficial magic to ourselves. ALWAYS REMEMBER THIS CREED.

Practical magic celebrates the belief that we are all a part of the "WEB OF LIFE," and that every independent entity is connected in the minutest ways to other entities by an imperceptible web of vibrations. When we perform a small, symbolic task, it is connected to the real object of our thought by these interlaced vibrations. Quite simply, the more we are in tune with these vibratory waves, the more we can effect changes (even if very small ones) on material events. If someone wishes us negativity, persistent, positive thought returned to them will, little by little, alter their negative feelings. If someone is ill, our bold, optimistic thought can alleviate their condition to some extent. If we are out of touch with others, setting our thoughts in motion can eventually cause a chain of response. Never let negative thought, or disbelief, dissuade you!

This book is an attempt to tutor those who are willing to make these vibratory connections in their lives, and to alter their course. Hopefully, along the way some lessons will emerge about "gaining wisdom"—recognizing what we may influence, and when to leave well enough alone. It is vital to understand this: it is sometimes crucial not to intervene in personal affairs. This is a subtle point, but should have been grasped by the time we reach the final pages.

Try to take each lesson in turn. If you are having a problem with your house, the temptation, I know, will be to rush ahead to chapter 12 and read just that, opting for a spell that will "solve" your domestic difficulty. However, this will represent only one small part of what you need to know to become fully cognizant of the practice of successful, powerful, responsible magic. Take the time and trouble to read the whole; by doing this you will become a powerful exponent of the craft and will save yourself much disappointment.

The building blocks of white magic are presented in each successive chapter, so that by the time you reach the end of the book you will have a full working knowledge of what is required to interchange various elements within your spell-making and to design yourself the perfect, appropriate spell to deal with any situation that is thrown at you. If you learn about each step in magic—the thought process, the right way to meditate and send thought waves, the different symbolic possibilities, incorporation of individual colors, the use of candles, scent, and so on—you will be able to recognize what is necessary to work any kind of magic, for any kind of situation ....always remembering the restrictions placed on you by the Wicca philosophy, of course!

Wicca celebrates the idea that we are all individuals, that we have personal rhythms and responses to what we meet with in life: it is, in fact, for this reason that spells can and should be very personalized. Apart from the philosophy of "harming none," there are no hard and fast rules in the practice of spell-making. We are fluid, organic, emotional beings, and we should use the colors, combinations, climatic conditions, emblems, music, and so on that heighten our individual senses. In other words, the intention of this book is to provide you with the reasons why certain elements are used in magic-making, to enlighten you as to methods of making your thoughts stronger and more focused for good "spelling," and to provide a (by no means exhaustive!) list of symbols, color meanings, and herbal and scent properties to work with under the aegis of each individual moon.

The rest is up to you: do what feels right. Work with your intuition, and follow the rhythms set in motion by your spell-workings. You will soon learn to be adept, but don't worry too much about what is "right" and what is "wrong." Your magic will be strongest if you prepare the ground thoroughly; it will make better sense if you understand the guidelines given in this book. Sometimes, however, you will have to be flexible—if, for instance, you are in a place without candles, or when the time is not absolutely the first choice by moon or weather, or if you are in a public place and have to perform the whole spell in your head! This cannot be helped.

The important creed I have laid out; the working tools are described in the chapters before you. Now, make your own magic from an informed choice, which I hope will be yours by the last pages of this book. Make yourself, and others around you, happier by spreading your magic.

This is the true meaning of being a "white witch." And now to the poetic journey...*Blessed Be.*

MASTER SPELL: **A MAGIC CIRCLE.** This is the most important precursor to powerful magic. The idea of the circle is to create a powerful zone into which nothing harmful can reach. From inside the 360 degrees, the powerful witch has control over any forces coming from any direction: her sphere of power reaches everywhere. Most importantly, the circle also prevents any curious lower spirits from entering into the magic-making and corrupting the results.

There are many variations on the construction of the magic circle. However, some of the descriptions derive from the Druidic tradition, which, it is widely believed, sometimes used a circle in connection with divine sacrifice. From the Wiccan creed of harming no one, and my grandmother's beautiful circle— which was literally a pool of light and accompanied all her incantations for healing heart, mind, and body—I draw my own preferred model for a magic circle from which to pour forth beautiful, powerful, enlightened thoughts. To do it justice, you may wish to use as many as forty or fifty candles for a circle about two yards in diameter! If this seems too extravagant, settle for thirteen, and place them equidistantly around your drawn circle.

YOU WILL NEED
At least 13 small candles in glass holders, either flame-red or white (or both); rose petals, or rose potpourri, to strew in the center, with a little rose oil added to intensify the fragrance; a handful of earth; a small dish of water; a small mirror; a birch leaf, or twig if it is winter; a twig or leaf from the appropriate tree for the moon/month in which you are performing this spell; 2 yards of flame-red ribbon.

MOON PHASE: *Full (birch moon, for the purist).*

Choose the area in which you are to create your circle carefully. It is best to use the floor area in a room where you will habitually perform your magic, or even your garden on a still night.

Standing in the center of the circle you will create, place the candles around it in a clockwise direction—no more than 18 in. apart, and much closer if you are prepared to buy more candles and create a really intense ring of fire. Still standing in the center, strew some rose petals or potpourri around your feet, and sprinkle with a little rose oil to make the scent very powerful. Step once outside the circle, and place in the north of it the earth, in the south of it the dish of water, and west of center the mirror, which you should first hold up to the moon for just a few seconds. Finally, place the leaf (twig), or leaves (twigs), within the circle.

As soon as you are ready to begin the magic ritual of cleansing and bringing in power to your art, girdle yourself with the flame-red ribbon and tie it at your waist with a large bow. Now raise your arms to the moon, entreating also the element of air to carry your thought waves, and draw down the strength and luminosity of the beautiful full moon into your circle. Allow the light to fill your own being, and feel your emotional tides rising with the moon's energy. Now bow once to the divine entity, and promise to make only magic that is good.

Starting in the north, light each candle in sequence, saying *"Blessed Be"* each time. It is wonderful to light the candles in an unbroken chain, using either a long match (these are worth buying for magic anyway) or a special taper. If you light the candles in a steady stream from beginning to end of the circle, you are enacting the drama of our being part of the "one life," which is itself a circle. Performing this spell, you are, effectively, opening yourself up to the vibratory force of all existence, and your own vibrations should be soft, rhythmic, and unobtrusive in performing the spell.

Once the circle is ablaze, stand to full height and feel yourself growing in power. Imagine a great shaft of light, drawn from around you, circling the room and embracing your body, sweeping up energy like a huge tornado and removing every apathetic thought and feeling of negativity you have had in that space. If you wish to send good feelings to another person at the same time as working your spell, let the beam loop gently around them too, sending powerfully good feeling with it. Concentrate your thoughts and energy until you feel a tangible electric force of heat and light surging through you, the circle, and the room. Warn all negativity off your territory. Release the beam, folding it into your mirror like a magic light which returns home to a treasure chest. The mirror will become your pool of portable light, and should be near at hand when you are performing demanding magic. It will keep you safe, and retains the magnetic impression of the light you have generated.

It is good manners to sit quietly in the center of the circle for a while, and bow your head. Try to tune in to the quietest exhalations of the earth and beings around you. This is a good preparation for clairvoyant feelings, love magic, and healing magic, where you are trying to get into the "mind-set" of another person. Breathe in the rose scent, and bring your energy back under your control. Your first and most important ritual of initiation is complete, and you may let the candles burn low or extinguish them. Untie the ribbon girdle, cup it in your hands, and show it to the moon. Now place the leaves or twigs, mirror, and ribbon in a cloth bag (of any color: choose one that you feel is personal). Eventually, this might also contain a knife (which was traditionally used to cut herbs, flowers, and boughs), a wand (cut from hazel when the sap is rising), and a piece of silver jewelry (or gold if you wish) which you may choose to wear for magic ceremony.

Leave your magic area respectfully, as you would any spiritual place. The day after you have made a magic circle, it is nice to place white or red flowers in a ring, in vases, in the same places as your candles stood. Leave them for a day or so, then place them together in a space that may become a permanent altar. This can be as informal as you like—one of the pleasures of magic life is to incorporate magic ritual into your everyday life in a way that others would not even notice. An interesting, avant-garde flower arrangement—with unusual flowers, in dramatic containers—is one way of achieving this. Place extraordinary blooms together on your dining, kitchen, or bedside table, and put a rose-scented candle somewhere nearby. *You will understand their significance!*

In later chapters, we will be looking at small variations to each master spell, which will subtly alter its relevance to the particular sphere or situation. However, there is *no* variation to the magic circle. It should be used as described, and coupled as necessary with any other spell to purify your environment first, and then initiate new life.

A GLOSSARY OF TERMS USED IN THIS BOOK:
Throughout the book you will come across various terms within spell-working which may not be clear to you unless you have read my earlier spell books. Here is a brief explanation of such terms.

"CHARGING WITH POWER." This will arise when you are asked to "charge" a magnet or metal object, even a candle, with "power" or light drawn from the sun or from the moon.

Hold the object in the light, and vividly imagine the energy from the particular source entering into the object and filling it with particles of light and positivity. If you are asked to draw the power of the sun or moon, or even the light from candles, into yourself to boost your own sense of positivity and energy, you must concentrate and try to "feel" the heat gradually filling your body—from the tip of your toes to the top of your head—so that you can then draw on this special celestial power.

"BREATHING IN" SCENT OR COLOR. This is to send greater force with your magic. Throughout the book you will find particular scents and colors tied to individual subjects, which will usually involve a colored candle, sometimes scented as well.

Inhale the "feeling" of the color, along with the scent if appropriate, by powerfully imagining the color entering your heart, lungs, head, and chest, spreading gradually through your body, diffusing a glowing, good feeling as it does so. This alters your vibratory rate and attunes you to the power of that particular color. Scent, of course, strengthens the effect.

"CLEANSING." This might be applied to your magic-working space, your home, or a car, or in fact you yourself. It is a procedure of purification achieved mentally; sometimes, again, with scent as a backup. Imagine white light pouring forth from the source of the sun, or a fire, or anything that you can associate with positive power and strength (this may again be a simple candle!). Concentrate your thoughts on the light until you can almost feel your own temperature rise, and then you must direct this light and heat to the area required. If the energy is required to cleanse a space, see the heat and light eddying around the area like a great whirlpool of white energy. Prolong the feeling for a few minutes—although you may feel quite drained later!

SENDING A MENTAL MESSAGE. You may be asked to envision someone, then send them a simple message in your magic-working, particularly in love magic or if someone is ill or away from you.

You will first have chosen appropriate colors/scents to work with, and sometimes music helps you to feel closer to someone special if it is a shared song or poignant piece. Then, imagine their face as vividly as you can, preferably at a happy moment; freeze their smile and look as though directed totally at you, then quietly and calmly imagine you are touching their body, or hands, or face truly as if they were right with you. When you have the feeling that "contact" has been made, say your simple words (out loud, if you prefer) and imagine their face/eyes/smile recognizing what you have said. Send them a feeling of sweetness (perhaps like a gentle kiss) and then imagine them surrounded by a real, physical, powerful halo of light. Your message is complete.

"EMBRACING" THE MOON, SUN, ETC. This may be to say "thank you" after a spell has worked, or it may be to draw a feeling of warmth into your physical body before working magic.

Literally hold your arms outstretched and imagine hugging the moon, stars, sun, or a light source like candles or fire. Feel love for the world, banish anger and distress, fill up your tank on the vastness of the world and all in it that's good.

"When
the clock strikes 13—anything can
happen"! The witches' year is based around the
thirteen moon cycles, so divides into thirteen "months," each
of which is ruled by a tree. The first moon, the moon of beginning, is
ruled by the birch, and in this first chapter we introduce the components
that are required to start practicing white magic. The elements of earth, air,
fire, and water are explained. We learn to work magic by the moon's clock and
discover how to weave magical ritual and thought into everyday life without

1: IN THE BEGINNING

drawing attention to it. The significance of colors, scents, and oils is touched upon,
although it will be further developed in each unfolding chapter, and we learn about
some of the tools of magic-making. We look at the calendar significance
of this first moon, covering the period late December to mid-January, and
Yule, the festival that falls in this period. Honoring this ancient festival
can increase all our luck and happiness in small things. The master
spell in this chapter draws blessings from the birch moon
and tree which if done once or twice a year will
bring joy, happiness and luck into your
life.

BIRCH MOON—MOON OF BEGINNING. Color: FLAME-RED. Scent: ROSE. Number: 1. We must begin at the beginning, and draw our first lesson in magic-making in partnership with the first Druidic moon and all her domain, for it is the moon that introduces us to the infancy of magic.

"I saw the new moon late yestreen
    Wi' the auld moon in her arm;
    And if we gang to sea, master,
    I fear we'll come to harm."
"SIR PATRICK SPENS"—ANONYMOUS

The birch tree, which Samuel Coleridge dubbed the *"lady of the wood,"* is associated with purification and the protection of children and dependants. The beautiful silvery appearance of the trunk has an affinity with the silvery moon and reflects the moonlight at night, giving the tree an ethereal, very magical dimension. Perhaps it is for this reason that the witch's broom— symbol of her power and magical energy—was made from birch twigs, and sweeping the area in which you will perform magical rites with the birch broom, or "besom," is a powerful way to influence the outcome of your spell-making.

HONORING THE BIRCH

We must now consider briefly the significance of the birch in the calendar, and ways to honor and celebrate both season and tree-spirit. The moon itself falls just after Yule (December 21), and runs from approximately December 25 to January 17. This means that New Year's is the festival associated with the birch moon, the first moon of the year, while the elder governs Yule itself (see chapter 13).

You can reasonably weave some old pagan Yule rituals into any other religious feasts that likewise straddle midwinter (midsummer in the southern hemisphere) and the turn of a new year—remember how the Yule log, wreath, and charms placed in the Christmas pudding, in England, to ensure a bountiful year ahead have been incorporated into the Christian observance of Christmas. Indeed, the correspondence between the Christian festival and Yule/New Year's could not be more apparent, as the old festival was an honoring of the "new life" of the sun, which is born immediately after the midwinter solstice, December 21, which is why Christmas Day was set at this same moment in the calendar.

Two adversaries battle for leadership at Yuletide: namely, the Oak King, who is the manifestation of the summery, waxing year, and the Holly King, who is the spirit of the waning, wintry year. Connections between the appearance and accoutrements of the Holly King—who drove a team of deer, the animal sacred to the Celtic gods and the Druids, and wore holly in his hat—and Father Christmas, or Santa Claus, are easy to make. Even the red candles we use at Christmas have a connection with the color of the first flame of the sun, and the color associated with the first, birch moon. Candles of this color—along with white, which symbolizes all unity and thus the full return and restart of the wheel of the year—often adorned the altars and feast tables in the Yuletide house, much as they do now. The birch, however, is the symbolic tree of renewal and purification, and you might include birch twigs in your Yule fires to deepen the tie between the dying year (elder) and the reborn year (birch). The beautiful birch is a goddess tree, slender and silvery, and a symbol of hope of the summer returning. When the tree bursts into foliage later in the year, keep a sprig as a talisman for luck, love, and protection, and wear it pinned to your coat on May Day, at midsummer, at Lammas (August 1) and again at Yule. As the birch tree is loved by the fairies, cherishing a birch twig or sprig may give the wearer help in seeing these folk.

WORKING MAGIC BY THE MOON'S CLOCK

The birch moon is also known as the MOON OF INCEPTION and falls immediately after Yule. The moon is measured from full, which is the zenith of its power. This means, too, that magic is worked from the full moon through a waning moon (a moon on its way from full to last quarter, or last quarter to the day before "new"), which is used to rid a situation of bad spirit or feeling; and then through the growing (waxing) moon, which is used to attract new, better, growing opportunities. Choose the timing of your magic-making very carefully…

THE MOON PHASE

If this is to be your first foray into spell-making, you should begin with a splash! Build up to your first magic: you need not wait for the birch moon in late December/early January, but it would be wonderful to start on a full moon, when the celestial body exerts its most powerful pull on the earth, its oceans, and all of us, whose being is so largely made up of water. Most calendars have moon information printed on the appropriate days, and the table at the end of this book see page 175) shows which moons fall when for the years 2000

to 2003. Check which moon will begin with the next full moon, and honor it in your magic-making with a twig from the appropriate tree, as well as a birch twig to signify your own beginning as a magic-worker.

If you are absolutely longing to start but have just missed a full moon, all is not lost. So long as you work with a waning moon for purification spells, you are still using the potent power of moon magic to rid yourself of anything negative. Always use a waning moon in any spell that banishes something—be it a wart or a smoking habit, weight loss, or a sweet ex-lover who cannot accept your new relationship (this last should be a very tender spell!). You should use the waxing moon only when you want to draw something *into* your life.

WEATHER

At times when you cannot use a full moon—wait for a storm! There is no more electric moment at which to launch your magic thought into the world than with the birth of a storm of rain and wind, and a ragged moon. You can bring these elements together in one extraordinary way, if you are lucky enough to see "the new moon with the old moon in her arms." This happens when the part of the moon covered by the shadow of the earth is seen through it—rimmed with a silver thread, in effect. In Scotland, for instance, this is regarded as an infallible portent of bad weather, and occurs just before the storm is about to break.

Keep beautiful, sunlit days for spells of healing and love: the gentle solar rays will soften your energy and transmit warmth automatically with your own message.

THE ELEMENTS. Our strong personal connection to all other matter can be achieved through our understanding that we are all made up of the four elements —EARTH, AIR, FIRE, and WATER—one or other in greater proportion than others. Fire is the principal element in magic for its connection with creativity and purification; Water is the other principal element, for as human beings we are made up more of water than of any other element; and then, too, it is the element of emotion! Earth is vital to magic, for it is our planetary home; and everything we wish to "reach" must reverberate through the air. Weave them all in.

FIRE

Fire is one of the crucial four elements, connected indissolubly with the "divine spark." Representative of the sun's life-giving energy, it has transfiguring powers. Light is connected with knowledge and a move away from fear; heat has the power to drive off illness and create mood and closeness with another being; and flame purifies, regenerates, and creates chemical changes. Fire changes raw food to cooked, removing much of its impurity, and fire applied to cold water gives us warm water in which to bathe. Quite simply, fire refines us.

By thinking in a concentrated manner over a candle, and then lighting it, we symbolically move our thought out beyond us, into the ether. The power of thought is the linchpin of magic, for it is through thought that we gain mastery over the situations and other life forms around us.

Part of the way in which magic works is by enacting an affinity between people and things. Lighting a sacred flame calls down a piece of the powerful sun to shine on a benevolent situation, or "burn up" destructive forces which are hindering individual progress. This lies at the heart of the magic flame circle of purification.

COLORS AND CANDLES

As the bringers of light and color and, sometimes, scent, candles are an essential part of magic-making. We are all familiar with the use of wax in images and figurines as part of the myth of witches' work, but the pure and untainted candle to which a thought and wish is attached is a powerful carrier of messages. It is important to have a wide range of candles available, for the many different purposes they fulfill in magic ritual. Keep a rainbow of colors, and always choose the color appropriate to the subject (you can check individual chapters for these). Always place a candle on your altar (see page 148) to correspond to the moon and month you are in, and work one or more colors in tandem as necessary.

For initiating magic, the color you need is flame-red. If you were trying, for instance, to precipitate some love interest for the first time with someone you like, you would use the red to initiate communication, and marry it to purple (for passion) or pink (for love), in addition to the appropriate color for the month.

For working steady magic, use votive candles in glass holders; these will burn for up to about eleven hours. If you buy "tea-lights" (very small candles that burn for just a few hours), you will have only a short time for your magic to work.

This is fine if you have a short spell to perform, or once you have become adept at sending your thoughts and getting quick results—in other words, after much practice. Until that time, use the longer-burning candles, to which you can return many times over several hours and re-send the thoughts of your spell. The use of "column candles" (the really big, church-style candles which can burn for days) and tapers, which we think of

as tapers, should be matched to particular spells. When you are burning a candle and working a spell over several days, and notching the candle in several places to mark each day's burning, a taper in the appropriate color is the right choice.

If you are selecting a candle for an altar—one that will last for several weeks or even remain indefinitely—use a pillar candle in white or beeswax, and add one smaller candle in the color appropriate to the moon and month.

SCENT

Many candles can now be bought with essential oils already incorporated into them, and this makes lighter work for a witch. Scent is vital in spell-making for several reasons: it alters the psychological state of the worker, bestowing confidence, for instance, or aiding concentration; it affects the mood of the recipient of magic in love or healing spells, relaxing them or reviving their spirits; and it reminds us of times and places that may be helpful to our focus, as well as working again on the affinities between people and things.

There is an equivalent olfactory "rainbow" which can and should be woven into magic, and each chapter in the book specifies the scent that corresponds to that moon and month. If you cannot find candles that are ready-scented with appropriate fragrances (*not* "ice-cream sundae" or "chocolate fudge"), you can instead anoint the candle yourself with oils (perfume or essential) from your storage cupboard. The easiest way to do this is to light the candle first and wait until the wax has become a little molten at the top. Extinguish the flame, add a few drops of oil to the wax and allow it to harden again, then re-light the wick. The same result can be achieved by softening the edges of the candle with a flame, rolling it in some oil, waiting for the wax to harden, and then lighting the candle.

For any magic purification ritual, rose is the absolutely essential oil. It should be burned with the candle—for extra effect, this can be in a burner alongside the candle on your altar. If you feel like creating a proper piece of theater, burn some rose potpourri on a charcoal burner or in a fireplace to cleanse and purify completely both the environment and any situation.

THE OTHER ELEMENTS

These will come under closer inspection in later chapters, but deserve a mention here.

WATER, the element of feeling, is used in the spell of purification and can be represented by placing clean river or rainwater in a silver or wooden dish beside your magic-working area, or on the altar. Some spells require that you go to water to perform them.

EARTH, the element of humankind (from which we are made, although we are made also from water) is crucial to the "grounding" of a spell—that is, making it real and not just wishful thinking. Some spells require symbolic burial to make use of earth; otherwise, a handful of earth, or plants grown in earth, will find their way into magic ritual.

AIR is all around us, and drawing our arms up or breathing steadily during magic-making will involve the air—the element of our thought. Some spells are best performed from a height to make full use of the air.

MAGIC IN EVERYDAY LIFE. As you begin to walk the path of Wicca philosophy, you will want to incorporate magic and spell-making into your daily life, but perhaps without drawing attention to it. Because spell-making is as fundamental to Wicca as the air that we breathe, finding an outward expression of magic will draw more power, merriment, and joy into your life. The aim is to bring a rainbow of colors into your life—perhaps without anyone else realizing—and subsequently find a *"pot of gold"* within your everyday existence.

OUTSIDE

OPEN YOUR HEART TO NATURE. Vow to think more about the natural world, and make your home (whatever its type) a haven for living things. If you live in an apartment, this will be somewhat restricted, but you can nevertheless make sure of keeping as many thriving potted plants, herbs, and flowers—of varied colors—close to as many sunlit windows as possible. Whenever you water them, simply say *"Blessed Be,"* and think warmly of all animated nature.

GO FURTHER: cast crumbs to birds from your rooftop, leave out old bread, even provide proper seed in suitable containers through the winter. If you have a garden, or a balcony, make a birdhouse or nesting box to encourage wildlife around your living quarters. A bird bath, or a water feature that will attract dragonflies and other watery life, brings the element of water to add to the element of air that your birdlife symbolizes. Thank the deity every day for these simple pleasures of sharing moments with other creatures and plants. Think of it as an offering to Mother Nature to place these items, which will attract her progeny, around your environment. Tie white and purple ribbons around your front-door knob, gatepost, or mailbox, or even your car steering wheel, to protect you and your loved ones and draw beneficence to your dwelling. Always feel a rush of color entering your life as you do this.

INSIDE

Make sure you have all the colors of the rainbow somewhere in your home. Venerate the element of fire with a constant candle flame or altar. Spread a cloth over a beautiful table or even an old box (either is fine) in any color that relates to the season, or tree/moon, or just your own mood. Place a cut flower in a glass vase (symbolizing light), or a growing plant in a small terracotta pot (symbolizing earth), on this altar, and light a candle for even just a few moments whenever you are at home. Always thank the spirit for small blessings, and look for some good in everything. This simple re-attuning of your thinking to a positive outlook should gradually draw powerful good fortune to you and those dearest to you. Think this through whenever you light your flame, or pot up herbs and flower seeds, or feed the birds, or water your greenery.

RIBBONS

You will be invited to incorporate ribbon—one of magic's most significant ingredients—not only into your everyday life in the most romantic of ways, but also into many of the spells described in this book. Ribbons symbolize the beauty of a cord with other people, and I like to tie ribbons around the letters and cards I send to symbolize an offered bond of welcome, or perhaps healing, or the need for swift response, in colors that reflect the particular situation. If you also place a few drops of an appropriate essential oil on the ribbon ends so much the better. You will find more detail about ribbons in each succeeding chapter, matching the concerns of the color and the subject.

Ribbons, then, can be tied around any object to draw magic into the situation. You will tantalize friends with questions about your decorative style if you tie a large golden yellow ribbon—which symbolizes both gatherings and celebration— around your dinner table. This is likely to lend a magic hand to the evening's proceedings, and your guest(s) will be "ENCHANTED." In addition to this, I usually buy fresh, growing herbs from the supermarket weekly and tie red ribbons around the pots or foliage. This initiates the magic vibration of the plants into the air and around my visitors. Sometimes I send every dinner guest away with an herb tied in this way, so that they take a little magic and love home with them.

ABOUND YOUR HOUSE OR OFFICE, OR EVEN IN YOUR CAR, TIE RIBBONS OF DIFFERENT COLORS.

- A silvery-colored ribbon or cord, tied around the telephone, will draw happy and positive communications from friends and associates.

- Tie a green ribbon around the faucets of your bathtub, so that as you soak you draw health, mental alertness, perfection, wisdom, love, and the ability to complete simple tasks calmly, into your mind, body, and spirit. Guests will also feel recharged when they go into your bathroom.

- Luck will attend you if you place sunshine-yellow candles or ribbons anywhere that money is kept: *tie a yellow ribbon around your checkbook, for example!*

- Send out cards and letters tied with a ribbon of any color to suit the situation: *green if your recipient is sick or tired, purple if you want to attract attention, pink if it's love, olive green for forgiveness, black or white for matters of destiny.*

- Tie a red ribbon around the herbs you grow on your windowsill, to spread love and happiness in your home and to increase the joy you experience from eating the herbs in salads and cooked dishes.

MASTER SPELL: TO DRAW BLESSINGS FROM THE BIRCH MOON AND TREE.

This is a simple spell to entreat joy and happiness to attend your life. It asks for nothing specific, although the concepts of renewal, hope, and infinite possibility are inextricably linked with the wishes herein. You may find that performing this spell only, once or twice a year, will circumvent the need for any spells that ask for something specific, for luck is drawn powerfully with this ritual.

This is a beautiful spell to do at any time when the birch holds sway. You should notice soon afterward that even the smallest tasks can be executed more expediently and that many things that are important to you seem to fall—magically—into place.

YOU WILL NEED
1 yard of red ribbon; a flame-red candle (choose a column or pillar candle this time, so that you may relight it for a few hours each day for 14 days—or, more correctly, nights); a long-stemmed red flower, or bouquet of flowers, placed in water; a wand cut from a birch tree (ask first!), no more than 12 in. long; a few drops of benzoin, frankincense, or rose oil, or all three (all purifying oils which also bring blessings).

MOON PHASE: *Full...or nearly so.*

At a quiet time, bow to the moon and ask attendance from the divine spirit. Tie the red ribbon into a bow around the base of the candle and place it next to the flower or flowers on a small table. Take the wand in your dominant hand and raise your arms to the moon. Make a pledge to notice, and be concerned for, nature in any small way. Widen this thought, by all means, to the most important element of it: the pledge ultimately to do more for those around you who need your help in any form, and in any way that you can give it, according to your means. In other words, promise to venerate the one life we share with everything, which is part of the divine spark.

Anoint the candle with oil and then light it; as you do so, close your eyes and think of all the life forms breathing quietly and imperceptibly around you. Ask for help in all things, and offer thanks for all the thoughts that bring a smile to your face. Ask especially for luck and love for the children around you, and promise to try to make them smile whenever you can. Every time you raise a smile on another's face, you please the divine spirit immeasurably.

Pass the wand through the flame and in an arc around the candle; then describe a circle around your working area with the wand, moving your whole body clockwise as you do so. Say simply, *"Blessed be all things; may I add to the harmony of the life force; hold me gently in the web of all creation. So mote it be!"* Lay the wand near the candle, sing, laugh, sit, relax, and think warm and even funny thoughts about yourself and those around you. After about an hour, blow out the candle and untie the ribbon, saying *"Blessed Be"* as you do so.

You are now ready to move on to the next phase of magic-making and tackle divination.

☽

CENTERED

ON THE ROWAN MOON—THE MOON OF VISION

AND ASTRAL TRAVEL—THIS CHAPTER EXPLORES THE SUBJECT

OF VISUAL SYMBOLOGY IN MAGIC. THE SIGNIFICANCE OF INDIVIDUAL

SYMBOLS THAT HAVE BEEN IN USE FOR CENTURIES IS EXPLAINED, SO THAT YOU

WILL BE ABLE TO SELECT PICTORIAL DEVICES RELEVANT TO ANY SITUATION FROM THE

LIST PROVIDED. THUS, THIS CHAPTER REVEALS THE IMPORTANCE OF PUTTING YOUR OWN

SIGNATURE ON YOUR MAGIC-MAKING, AND SHOWS YOU HOW TO BEGIN TO DO SO. THE MASTER

SPELL CONCERNS ASTRAL TRAVEL AND CLAIRVOYANCE, SO THAT WE CAN START THE PROCESS

2:VISION

OF EMPTYING THE MIND OF BRIC-A-BRAC AND OPENING

IT TO INSPIRATIONAL POWER; THOSE WHO ARE QUICK

LEARNERS WILL ALREADY BE BEGINNING TO RECEIVE CLAIRVOYANT FLASHES ABOUT THEIR LIFE

AND FUTURE. THE "VARIATION" SPELLS INCLUDE ONE THAT EMBRACES ORDINARY TRAVEL—

SETTING OUT ON A CAR JOURNEY, OR MAKING THE GRAND TOUR—AND IS THE WITCH'S EQUIVALENT

OF WEARING A ST. CHRISTOPHER MEDAL. WE LOOK AT THE CALENDAR SIGNIFICANCE

OF THE ROWAN MOON, WHICH INCLUDES THE FEAST DAY OF IMBOLC, ABSORBED INTO

THE CHRISTIAN CALENDAR AS CANDLEMAS. THIS IS NOT A POWERFUL MOMENT OF

EARTH ENERGY, BUT THE FIRST SIGNS OF LIFE ARE BEGINNING

TO APPEAR IN THE FORM OF CROCUSES, DAFFODILS,

AND SNOWDROPS. THE EARTH IS STARTING

TO STIR...

ROWAN MOON—MOON OF VISION AND ASTRAL TRAVEL. Color: RUBY or PINK-GOLD (colors of the winter sunset). Scent: GERANIUM. Number: 2. Visualization is a serious notion in the performance of magic and spells. Based on the contention (long held in Hindu tradition) that thoughts are the beginning of all actualization, visualizing any desired end very crisply will—ultimately—produce the materialization of that vision. Thus, the more precisely a vision can be formulated, and then held, the more perfectly will that vision become reality.

"And Winter, slumbering in the open air
  Wears on his smiling face a dream of Spring!"
"WORK WITHOUT HOPE"
SAMUEL TAYLOR COLERIDGE

Central to visualization are the rowan tree and moon. Part of the connection is possibly to do with the weather that occurs around the time of the rowan moon, in early February. At this time—of frosts and silent nights, clear, icy skies, and frozen ground—there is a timelessness and a stillness which lend themselves naturally to the gentle internal rhythms of the psychic brain. Then, too, the earth stirs into a vision of reawakening, and the first flurry of early bulbs appears. This is a metaphor, of sorts, for the seeds of knowledge and actual being of our future, which lie quiet and almost undisturbed within our subconscious until they blossom forth into colorful symbols of what will come.

Hence, the festival of Imbolc—taken from the Celtic word "imelc," meaning ewe's milk, and thus symbolic of the first few lambs of the season fed by the ewes—is a celebration of "first stirrings" and an appropriate moment to look ahead to the unfolding year. To the careless eye, there is nothing to see;

to the trained eye, there is astonishing proof of new hope and life. If you can, plant snowdrops—even in your window boxes—to await this special moment.

If you would become an adept witch, learn the art of visualization well. The effort you make will be rewarded with an evocation to match your dream; but, of course, as always, dream (or wish) wisely!

CELEBRATING IMBOLC
The festival of IMBOLC celebrates the transformation of winter into earliest spring: the movement away from the sway of the crone (old woman, deep winter) toward the virgin goddess (early spring).

The Christianization of this festival coincides with Mary taking the infant Christ-child to the temple for purification, where she was told that he would be a "light unto the world." For this reason, the Christian festival of Candlemas (symbolizing the light) was absorbed into the pagan feast day, which actually occurs on February 2. The Celtic world recalls the honor of Brigid, or Briide, the pagan earth goddess, at this time.

CORN DOLLIES were the trappings of the goddesses of early spring. If you wish to bless your home, office, or bedchamber in the old way, make a corn dolly, burn candles to honor the spring spirit, and plant your spring seedlings with a short invocation to the goddess for the fruitful realization of your wishes. Also, give thanks for all blessings bestowed thus far in the year.

CORNBREAD CAKE is connected with the festival and is simple to make. It is also a good cake for taking on journeys, so you can fulfill a dual purpose here.

YOU WILL NEED
4 tablespoons of cold butter; 1/2 teaspoon of salt; 1 cup of flour; 2 cups of cornmeal; 3 teaspoons of baking soda; fresh herbs (choose from rosemary, thyme, marjoram, and parsley); a little sugar; 1 cup of milk.

Rub the butter and salt into the flour and cornmeal with the baking soda until it has the texture of breadcrumbs. Add the herbs and sugar, and toss lightly. Make a well in the center and add the milk, combining with the dry ingredients until all the liquid is incorporated. Knead very lightly, shape into a rough round, and slit a "cross" through the middle (effectively quartering the bread, but not right through: it will pull apart easily when baked). Place in a greased and floured round cake pan and bake at 400°F for half an hour. It will keep fresh for several days.

ROWAN-BERRY WINE honors both calendar and festival, but you will need to use rowan berries picked the previous fall. The berries are bright red and look lovely in wine.

YOU WILL NEED
1 quart of rowan berries; elderflower syrup to taste; juice of 1 large or 2 small lemons; a small piece of ginge root; a pinch of saffron; sugar; yeast.

Steep the berries in 1 quart of water. Boil gently, then add the elderflower syrup, lemon juice, gingerroot, and saffron, and leave to macerate for a week to ten days. Strain, and add a scant 1 cup of sugar per quart of liquid. Add yeast, following the brewing instructions on the package. Ferment in tightly corked bottles, and allow the flavor to develop (this will take a minimum of a week). Be wary—this quickly becomes a very potent brew indeed. If you cannot get rowan berries to make wine, choose an unusual homemade wine such as ginger wine and toast the prosperity you expect in the waxing year.

COLORS. In this moment of late winter, draw in the magnificent rich golds and ruby hues from the cloud-softened winter sunsets, so intense in color, and place the magic of the fire inside your home.

RIBBONS in these colors should be garlanded everywhere to pep up your psychic energy. Arrange exotic blooms from this color spectrum in your kitchen, and lay a permanent place at the table with glass plates or mats and linen in these shades. This is particularly important if you are trying to visualize a relationship with someone moving into the realm of partnership—for the number 2, connected with this second moon of the year, is concerned with pairing and cooperation.

SPREAD YOUR MAGIC AROUND. Send cards to single friends who would like to feel the stirring of love, and choose an envelope or ribbon to tie around it in pink-gold hues. If a lonely friend has a birthday at this time of year, choose a gift with color as the principal thought: perhaps ruby goblets, or a box of beautiful candles in the right shade.

For yourself, burn a candle continuously (or nearly so) to attract cooperation from family, friends, business associates, and lovers. Go for color again, but combine this with the scent of geranium (and possibly rose also), for this fragrance has the power to aid emotional healing, meditation, and self-awareness—all of which fall within the domain of the rowan moon.

It is also a great boost to pleasure, color, and playful magic to tie small clusters of ruby-red carnations and hide them in unexpected pockets of your clothes, around the house, or in the car. Revive the Victorian tradition of a living flower fastened into a silver vase and pinned to a jacket, and fasten bouquets onto your purse, briefcase, and rear-view mirror. In this way, you are drawing luck and the power of vision into your daily life.

SYMBOLOGY IN MAGIC: Symbols are an ancient part of magic rite and practice, used for their capacity to recall to mind certain predominant aspects of people, relationships, or circumstances. Their use in spell-making is an obvious aid to visualization; choosing the right visual metaphor can help you to send very clear messages into the world about yourself, or to the person or event you have in mind.

Symbols also play a crucial role in divination, and many oracles employ a simple symbolic system to find the right answer to the querist's questions—the tarot is one particular manifestation of a symbolic language. What is important is that you feel comfortable with the symbolic language you choose to employ. The symbols are just tools of your own psyche, and you must direct them—not the other way around!

Having said that, certain symbols have age-old credence in the language of magic, and you could start with some of these and then add symbols that appeal to your own conscious mind.

In BEWITCHED I gave a fairly full glossary of symbols used in love magic, so here I concentrate on the subjects explored in each chapter of this book and give suggestions for the most easily acquired talismans, or those with the strongest history and mythology.

In all your magic-working, choose the symbols that appeal and have the most personal relevance, then combine them with any other instructions given in the master spells to arrive at a signature spell, which should solve any elements of a personal nature you want to incorporate into your magic-making.

BEGINNINGS

These symbols are suitable for use in spells to begin a love affair, find a small first house, boost your baby-making potential, inaugurate a business, or start the first day at a new job or educational establishment. The following are useful to wish luck and positivity on any beginnings: SPIDERS initiate the web of vibration: these are very lucky creatures, and will bless your beginnings. ACORNS symbolize the tiny beginning from which great and enduring projects may grow. For the Druids, acorns were also connected with immortality. The acorn is perhaps the most powerful single symbol in any magic. The CAMPION flower is a symbol of the first stirrings of love, or at the very least, some interest! LILAC is also a flower used to symbolize the first love. A BELL signifies the first wish to gain someone's attention. It can be used to make an appeal to be heard—in business or relationships. The NEW MOON is symbolic of a sacred start. The BIRCH tree and birch broom are symbols of the wish to start something properly and see it through.

VISION *and clairvoyance*

The POPPY is a symbol of hypnotic power, dream prophesy, and visions of paradise. PEACOCK FEATHERS are frightening to some witches (my grandmother included) because of their supposed connection with the *"evil eye."* A refusal to be worried by this potent symbol will result in the power of vision being granted to the querist. The RAINBOW is the arc of communication with the gods—thus, a symbol of inspired communication and vision. Re-creating the rainbow around your house will boost your clairvoyant capacity and ensure good luck. The STAG is a symbol related to clairaudience, because of the stag's sharp sense of hearing. A SPYGLASS signifies the wish to have inside information on an unrevealed situation. The mirror is similar, but is also used for self-revelation. The UNICORN bestows the power to see fairy folk!

LOVE *and feeling*

FLOWERS are the symbol of hope in love. Flora brings the spring flowers, thus awakening love and hopes of joy. MYRTLE symbolizes fidelity. The SWAN is the bird of Venus; MUSICAL INSTRUMENTS are the messengers of love. The APPLE is the most powerful love talisman, along with the ROSE—the attribute of Venus, and thus of true love. An ARROW kindles love and takes a message sent in thought.

A FOUNTAIN symbolizes a garden of love; put one anywhere in your house or garden to draw love to you. CUPIDS have an age-old connection with love. The OAK is the favorite Druidic symbol of lasting love. A CARNATION symbolizes engagement, a KEY a most important love, and a KNOT an indissoluble bond. PEONIES relate to forgiveness in love, and the PANSY is the best flower for love potions and spells!

WORK *and business*
The BEE is a symbol of hard work. CLOVER signifies plenty and good fortune. A THIMBLE means patient work. GOLD RIBBON is symbolic of the bond and commitment to good work with good reward. BRICKS signify solid foundations. An ANT symbolizes work in a community, a SPINNING WHEEL working from home, a LADDER upward ascent and progress in business. COINS are symbolic of gain! The ALDER is the tree of completeness and utility. A SNAIL: working steadily, without rush; SPADE: working with the earth; BIRDS: working toward good of others; SCYTHE or sickle: working with the earth's bounty.

ENCHANTMENT *and passion*
A WILLOW KNOT is a powerful enchanter's tool and symbolic of enchanted, passionate love. HAIR also symbolizes passionate love, and is used to enchant. The CAT is the enchanter's animal, along with the HARE. LILIES (especially tiger lilies) are the flowers of passionate embrace. YARROW is the witch's herb of enchantment and can be used in a love nosegay. A MAGNET

is a symbol of powerful attraction, a WEB enchantment, and a crucible or CAULDRON the witch's power. THREAD signifies power over fate. A RED ROSE, naturally, represents passion. The PESTLE AND MORTAR are instrumental in empowerment, and are used in making love spells.

DISENCHANTMENT
All of the above, wrapped around with HAWTHORN. CAMPHOR BALLS: symbols of deterrence; YARROW (herb): used in a way opposite from above, for arresting evil thoughts; a GARLIC bulb: antiseptic, so again, good for refusing bad thoughts from another person; a THORN: slowing progress; a PADLOCK: to refuse access; a "stop" sign!

STRENGTH *and security*
The ACORN (see Beginnings) is a symbol of inner power and determination to become greater. HAIR symbolizes the strength of another in your hands (use wisely). DIAMOND is the hardest and most enduring stone. The number SEVEN is connected with strength: seven sticks are an old symbol of unity, which precludes individual weakness. A HAMMER signifies personal strength and wisdom. The OAK LEAF is a symbol of the tree of strength and wisdom.

ENCIRCLEMENT *or reversal*
A MAGNET; also HOLLY sprigs, measuring COMPASS: designating a new circle; a HAND: normally shown palm upward, use this time palm down; upside-down TABLE: the tables turned; CLOCK and key: symbolic of

starting over again with a new cycle; a FIGURE EIGHT; things in a perpetual state of flux.

WISDOM *and knowledge*
A BOOK is a symbol of dedication to learning and material as yet unknown. A MAGIC WAND made of hazel is symbolic of ancient knowledge from Mercury. A TREE signifies flourishing; traditionally, this is the apple, sometimes olive, but in Wicca, the HAZEL. The OWL knows the unknown, nighttime things! CANDLES or a LAMP are symbolic of enlightenment. The SNAIL symbolizes slow degrees of gain and perfection, or patience to learn; a SCROLL or STYLUS: signifies preparedness to listen and learn. The SNAKE is connected with wisdom. A MULBERRY TREE: symbol of prudence.

CELEBRATION *and feasting*
The CORNUCOPIA (horn of plenty). Fruit symbolizes the completed harvest and time to unwind. BRAIDS OF RIBBONS, as in a May dance, signify joyfulness everywhere! The HARP is the celebratory instrument. VINE LEAVES are entwined for celebratory thanks. FLOWERS symbolize the earth's thanks and celebration. GOLD-COVERED AND SILVERED ALMONDS, as used in weddings, symbolize buoyant celebration—and fertility!

RESILIENCE *or survival*
TREES or a forest are symbols of great depth and self-reliance. BLOSSOMS signify that new life is being produced. The HORSESHOE is symbolic in the same way as a magnet

but is luckier. A WISHBONE represents ancient luck. GARLIC cloves symbolize the ability to fight off any pestilence and ill thought. An IVY LEAF: medical connections and tenacity. The LYRE charms away any threat. The UNICORN (and horn) is a symbol of resilience to all evil. The HEDGEHOG: resilience in general. WINGS (or an angel figure) represent victory over adversity.

HEARTH *and home*
DOLL-SIZED FURNITURE is symbolic of domestic peace; a MODEL HOUSE is similar. SHELLS signify bliss and beauty in the home, a CANDLE HOLDER and FIRE warmth at the center of the house. A BEEHIVE and HONEYCOMB mean a honeyed life in the house. A SPIDER'S WEB: an enchanted realm, made by the persistence of the homemaker; the four elements contained in one space: symbolic of complete riches within the home. THATCHING REED tied around with beautiful ribbon: symbolic of "joy under this roof."

COMPLETION *and finishing tasks*
A WREATH, full circle, RING or measuring COMPASS—all for obvious reasons. A tied-off KNOT: no loose ends. A DOCUMENT TIED IN A PILLOW WITH RIBBON: any paper-work can be used in this way to show you are determined to put it to "bed"; a large black DOT: a symbolic period.

TRAVEL *and foreign affairs*
SHELLS, SEAHORSES, SAILS, BOATS, and SAND all symbolize something foreign. GRASSHOPPERS often indicate that someone will travel shortly.

MASTER SPELL: **ASTRAL TRAVEL.** This master spell teaches astral projection, which is a meditative state often helpful to clairvoyant vision. It is also possible literally to "visit" someone and impart an important message, make an apology, or prepare them for some important news or event.

The ingredients of the famous witches' "flying ointments" included hemp, magic mushroom combined with belladonna, and monkshood steeped in tallow. But beware! The herbs that formed the basis of these ointments are dangerous to use, and really must not be handled today—you might become a great witch, but you wouldn't be around for long! For the modern initiate, the heavily drugging herbs that caused hallucination have been replaced by gentler medicines.

YOU WILL NEED

About 2/3 fl. oz. of almond oil, to which are added 3 drops each of vervain, patchouli, and frankincense; or frankincense, basil, and cinquefoil; or geranium, juniper, and lavender oil; some music; a small glass of white wine (not too cold), steeped with borage flowers or leaves; a large pink-gold candle; a pink-gold ribbon.

MOON PHASE: *Any.*

Set the scene carefully. If you are not comfortable bathing in the mixed oils or massaging a little onto your body, then simply use room fragrances to distribute the scent and induce the hypnotic feeling of these meditative herbs. Sit calmly, breathe in the fragrances, and listen to the music playing very softly. Sip some of the wine very slowly: borage has a very euphoric impact on the senses, so don't hurry the feeling. It is wonderful to do this spell scantily clad, but near a fire. However, modest witches need not worry about this. The most important thing is that you be comfortable, secure, and warm!

Light the candle. Tie the ribbon around your waist and lie back. Imagine the energy spreading from your feet, right through your body, in slow waves, and think of this energy in terms of scent, sound, and warmth drawn from around you. The wine may help to spread the glow! Move the energy very slowly: take at least half a minute to reach your knees, then likewise your hips and chest. Feel the fire spreading, and listen to your breathing. Let your mind float free, as if you were undergoing self-hypnosis. When the warmth, light, and sound have reached your head, imagine yourself free-falling through the universe and feeling utterly safe.

Now, still vaguely aware of the ribbon that anchors you to yourself, drift, and imagine you are angelic, powerful, gentle, and strong, and that you can visit whomsoever you wish. Go slowly: take them a message. In your mind's eye, look them in the eye and tell them anything you want. If you are preparing for a significant event, imagine yourself going through all the motions in a kind of rehearsal.

When you have had enough, imagine you are pulling gently on the ribbon, bringing yourself back to the closer realm of the music, scent, and heat. Wake yourself gently, and as you do, feel your limbs again. Listen to your breathing. Take mental note of anything you learned. You will be able to make wise use of this information.

VARIATIONS ON THE MASTER SPELL

IF YOU WANT TO SCRY (the old term for divination) rather than travel, follow the steps of the spell until you tie the ribbon around your waist, then take a little of the melted candle wax and toss it quickly into iced water just as you ask a question: the wax shape supplies the answer. Some people are very astute at reading these shapes, and you will find them much more suggestive than tea leaves!

IF YOU WANT TO TRAVEL SOMEWHERE TOTALLY PHYSICAL (none of the astral) and do a spell to ensure success, scatter the oils on the vehicle that will take you there, be it car, plane, or boat—make this very discreet in the latter two cases— and wear your ribbon underneath your clothes.

IF YOU WANT TO DREAM A PROPHETIC DREAM and dream yourself into a certain place (perhaps to understand things better in order to protect yourself), sprinkle your chosen oils on your pillow about an hour before bedtime, tie the ribbon around your wrist, drink a little wine, and count yourself backward from 13 to 1, feeling warm and positive all the time. As you slide down into the dream world, ask that you remember all that is important in the morning. You can formulate a specific question in this way, and when you wake at any time during the night, write down any word that comes to you, or quickly record any picture. It will have sound advice to offer.

If you want to use the master spell to prepare your mind for receptivity, do the spell as described and then breathe in your chosen oils again while going over any information you are trying to remember once you have woken up. In this way, you will take in the facts in a calm, receptive, and dreamy state.

If you want to do this spell before reading the tarot or asking oracular advice, place your cards or book in the room near you, and when you have completed the spell, take the ribbon from your waist and tie it around the book or cards for half an hour before you do a reading. You will thereby achieve tremendous accuracy and clairvoyant perception.

You can use your chosen oils to ensure that you relax for a good night's sleep and empty your mind of all the daily accumulation of tension and minutiae that clog up your rest. Simply sprinkle the oils on or under your pillow (without candle, ribbon, or music), close your eyes, and experience the gentle sensation of energy moving over your body from toe to head. Do this every night!

Whenever you travel "long haul," wrap up the oils and candle with the ribbon and put them into your luggage to ensure a safe journey. Also, sprinkle the oils on the foreign pillow you must dream upon.

)

WATER

IS THE MEDIUM OF FEELING. FOR MANY

PEOPLE, THE LIFTING OF A DEPRESSED OR SADDENED STATE

CAN BE EFFECTED SIMPLY BY PADDLING IN WATER, THEREBY RECHARGING

THE EMOTIONAL BATTERIES. SO PREDOMINANT IS WATER IN OUR COMPOSITION,

THAT OUR VERY ESSENCE SEEMS TO BE MADE OF THIS ELEMENT—AND THUS, BY

IMPLICATION (IF THE ANCIENTS KNEW ANYTHING), ARE WE MADE FOR LOVE. FOCUSED ON THE

ASH MOON—THE MOON OF WATERS—THIS CHAPTER EXPLORES THE REALM OF FEELING. THE

COLORS, SCENTS, HERBS, FLOWERS, AND SYMBOLS THAT RELATE ESPECIALLY TO LOVE ARE

3 : LOVE

EXPLAINED, AND WE DISCOVER HOW TO BUILD AN INDIVIDUAL SPELL FOR ANY PROBLEM OF THE HEART. THUS THE MASTER

SPELL IS A LOVE SPELL, WITH INTERCHANGEABLE ELEMENTS THAT CAN BE ARRANGED TO

SUIT THE NEEDS OF A PERSONAL SITUATION. AS IN THE PREVIOUS CHAPTER, HOWEVER, THE

INTENTION IS TO SHOW YOU HOW TO MAKE ALTERATIONS TO *any* OF THE ELEMENTS AND IMPOSE

YOUR OWN SIGNATURE ON YOUR MAGIC. WE AGAIN LOOK CAREFULLY AT RIBBONS AND

CORDS, AND AT THE PROPER CHOICE OF CANDLE, AND PRESENT VARIOUS OPTIONS THAT

CAN BE WOVEN INTO EVERYDAY LIFE TO IMPROVE THE QUALITY AND STRENGTH

OF A LOVE BOND WITHOUT ANYONE ELSE KNOWING THAT THE MAGIC

IS BEING WOVEN! NO FESTIVAL FALLS IN THIS PERIOD,

BUT ST. VALENTINE'S DAY OCCURS JUST

BEFORE.

ASH MOON—MOON OF WATERS. Colors: CHERRY-PINK, AMBER. Scent: NEROLI, JASMINE, ROSE ATTAR. Number: 3. There is some confusion here. In pure numerology, the number 6 governs "pure love," while the number 3 is associated with social life, and very often with the appearance of a third member in the family—i.e. children. However, in the ancient tarot, the number 3 represented the couple with divine guidance, to make the perfect, divine marriage; today, this is seen as the couple and God.

"Mann und Weib und Weib und Mann
Reichen an die Gottheit an."

"Man and wife, and wife and man
  Reach towards the divinity."
  "THE MAGIC FLUTE"
  MOZART's own revisions to Schikaneder's libretto

It is this striving for a perfected union that we are dealing with here, whereas in chapter 6 we will address the difficulties that often attend love—such as fear of it, failure in it, and hindrance from others concerning it.

Without question, it is the moon of waters—of *feeling*—that is the moon concerned with love. In line with this, we are aiming at creating, with magical awareness, a union without malice, selfishness, or dominance. The most important step toward this is recognition of the motives that sometimes lead us away from this ideal; and then, too, we must recognize social responsibility within a partnership. A powerful couple of beneficent intention can have an ameliorative impact on those closest to them—not least by example.

So, how is it possible to attain this "divinity"—to continue to delight and surprise and spark the imagination of the one we love, years after the first gloss of a love affair has passed? How can we create a magical relationship, and discover the transfiguring power of a special union with one person who understands us completely, and we them? Is it possible to find, not just our "other half"—for this implies that we are only half a being on our own—but rather, our "extended self"?

The magic of a relationship begins, perhaps, with the recognition that it takes plenty of work, enthusiasm, and imagination to keep it healthy. Our post-Freudian concern with the Self has in some ways led us to expect that a partner must please us, forgetting our reciprocal obligation. We need to address the reality of our own necessary contribution. Equally, of course, we must also stop and assess a relationship with a partner who is doing all the taking—where our own input is out of all proportion and we feel abused. Recognition of these two basic tenets will help you immeasurably in deciding what magic is required: indeed, what is even justified!

There is no specific festival for this period, but you may wish to celebrate Valentine's Day for a week, rather than just one day, to draw out the love festival into greater meaning.

THE RAINBOW OF COLOR IN LOVE MAGIC. And so to the practice of magic in our love lives.…Here, you must draw on a veritable rainbow of colors in order to decide which aspects of love you are trying to appease. Keeping the cherry-pink theme behind all your magic-making (or rose-pink if you have lost all hope of ever being happy, or if you have had a lifetime of failures in love, see chapter 6), you will find that different aspects of love require different partner colors. In conjunction with the number 3, always choose three colors to work with in love, thereby aspiring to the "divine union."

- If selfishness has been your problem and, bravely, you can recognize this, incorporate the first color, FLAME-RED, into your love magic. This will symbolize the need to go beyond the first principle (you) and reach toward others; that first color will also in some ways represent you, keep it as your signature color until you no longer feel that selfishness is your handicap. This, of course, is equally true for your partner: if the person you love is conditioned to selfish behavior, try using flame-red to symbolize them, and move on to a more sharing color (such as pink-gold) when that ego begins to take a back seat!

- If you are looking to test a relationship's possibilities for moving into real partnership (as opposed to its being perhaps a mere fling), choose PINK-GOLD or RUBY-RED, colors for "pairs." This way, two of the colors in your love spell would

be pinks: cherry-pink for love, and pink-gold for partnership.

- If you aspire to marriage itself (the ceremony), the color for marriage and families is INDIGO or BLUE. If your bond is wondrous, but you are trying to find out whether it will ever make it to the altar, two of your colors will be cherry-pink (divine love) and blue or indigo (marriage).

- And the most needed color in love magic? PURPLE, WISTERIA, and LAVENDER are the shades that concern the passions! If you love your partner to bits, but there is simply not enough physical fun, this is your color.

- If you want to overcome the possibility of anything (perhaps the appearance of a potential rival) hindering your happy bond, work magic between you and your love including the color ROSE-PINK—to

which I would add WHITE, for the fulfillment of your wishes and hopes. Three tapers in three shades (choose from those given above), would help to weave gentle, healing thoughts into a worried mind.

- To advance your love affair to higher realms of security, or to share projects of an intellectual nature together—even, perhaps, to strengthen a loving relationship with someone whose intellect and mental powers you respect hugely—the color of strength, security and intellectual analysis is BRICK-BROWN. This would be the right choice for a relationship that has weathered the years with grace, and that you want to keep going strong. It would equally be the correct choice for a relationship with a university professor.

- If your lover has hurt you, or you them, and forgiveness is required,

burn one CHERRY-colored candle next to an OLIVE or GREEN candle, and perhaps add ROSE-PINK.

- If you have all you need, but wish for a truly enlightened, master association with your "extended self," surround your love with SILVER, WHITE, or GOLD and your love colors. All these colors respect superior intention.

- If your love relationship is merely waiting for a little cash injection to remove the tensions (or pay for a wedding, or a house, perhaps?), burn a golden, sunshine YELLOW candle with two others in your chosen love colors to attract material blessings to the union. This might also be your choice if you have fallen for some-one who works at the stock exchange or in a bank, or who is obsessed with money to the exclusion of romance. *Do you begin to see how you can play with colours to suit the situation?*

THE SCENT OF LOVE. According to Greek legend, when Venus was born, roses appeared in the world with her. The beautiful and famous Botticelli painting celebrates this, with Zephyr blowing a shower of pink roses from the breeze that wafts Venus to shore.

Subsequently, the rose has become an absolute icon for lovers, and it would be churlish to look further than this flower for the principal scent for love. What is fascinating is how many times the scent, rose attar, appears in aromatherapy charts in connection with any uplifting of the senses. We certainly understand better now the connection between the nose and the brain, and the ability of an essential oil to trigger memory, emotion, sexual feelings, learning, and healing—although a *precise* explanation may require many more tests, for many years to come.

For the purposes of magic, it may be enough to say that inhaling rose has a cheering, positive effect on the inhaler. Some cultures have similar relationships with neroli (orange blossom, sacred to marriage in India, for instance) and jasmine (renowned as a love tonic throughout the East and the South Pacific). I would personally add gardenia to this, although it can be difficult to find. Many of these scents have a proven powerful impact on our feelings of passion, as well as of contentment; in any case, few people could be impervious to the delicious fragrances of these wonderful flowers.

In her wonderful "bible" of aromatherapy, *The Fragrant Mind,* Valerie Ann Worwood cites the use of rose in blends for contentment, creativity, happiness, joy, peace, improved performance, and against emotional abuse, among others. In fact, whenever the perfume element has been fundamental to the magic, rose has featured as the key ingredient in love spells for many centuries. So, make this the first scent you buy for love spells of the twenty-first century!

HERBS AND FLOWERS IN LOVE. Herbs are powerful plants. Follow the instructions carefully; if you are pregnant, we recommend extreme caution in the use of herbs of any kind. In fact, if you are sensitive to food products generally, you should seek professional advice before using herbs at any time.

Why and how can herbs affect our emotional state? Will the use of dried lavender, or fresh pansy flowers added to salads, say, make any difference to our happiness in a relationship?

Herbs have weathered thousands of years of climatic change and adapted to a wide range of conditions—adaptations made possible by their complex chemical structure.

Handled properly, these chemicals can in turn help us as individuals to adapt to difficulty and change. This is the basis of herbal medicine—and problems of an emotional or psychological kind are in many ways indivisible from physical problems. There is therefore a genuine physical component to the use of herbs in magic—for they affect us physically.

WILD PANSY (*Viola tricolor*, not the hybrid pansies available from garden centers) relieves pain and promotes healing, cleanses toxins from the system, and is acordial for the heart. Used (in small doses) in magic spells, it has a positive effect on our physical and psycho-emotional states. Symbolically, it represents the one we have "thoughts" of—hence "pansy," from the French *pensées*, meaning thoughts.

The **VIOLET** is closely related to the pansy, and is another herb perennially appealing in love magic. Now believed to be beneficial in anti-cancer treatment, violet combats exhaustion and nervous skin conditions, has a pleasant taste in wine and sweets, and was incorporated in love potions and massage creams. Again, the flowers can be used in salads, and may have a tonic effect, leading to a loving feeling.

VERVAIN (verbena) is used for love philters and as the basis of love potpourris. This herb is excellent for nervous complaints, which might explain its benefit in emotional terms—a relaxed soul is always more attractive to a potential admirer! Vervain also stimulates the uterus, making women feel quite sensual. *But do not use during pregnancy.*

BORAGE has a reputation for lifting the spirits and inducing a natural euphoria. Wine made from borage (or steeped with it) has long been held to "make men and women glad and merry" (John Gerard, *The Herball*, 1597); it has been recommended as an addition to salads and also gives a certain *je ne sais quoi* to cakes and teas, in terms of both the flavor and the spiritual! At the very least, modern herbalists attribute antidepressant properties to the herb.

YARROW (milfoil) is the age-old divinatory herb, used in the regime accompanying questions to the Chinese oracle the *I Ching*. It is a relaxant and can lower blood pressure; also has a history of use for menstrual complaints. Add it to potpourris, especially for the bedroom.

ALCHEMILLA (lady's mantle) is the "little magic" herb, known for its alchemical connection. It can also be used in a variety of ways to treat female disorders, primarily heavy periods. It symbolizes the woman in love, and water collected from within its leaves is powerful in magic.

ARTEMISIAS are many and varied. They are too poisonous to use internally, and should always be handled with care. Grow a little southernwood (*Artemisia abrotanum*)

in the garden to attract "lad's love." Another artemisia, wormwood, was the basis for absinthe and vermouth, but its use is now restricted.

PERIWINKLE (*Vinca*) is another herb connected with the control of female problems. It is known to reduce blood pressure, and was called "sorcerer's violet" in reference to its power in love potions.

LADY'S BEDSTRAW (*Galium verum*) was made into an ointment with tallow, said to be a great relief for the aching limbs of weary travelers. The herb was also strewn for its odorous effects on lifting the spirits in the bedchamber!

LOVAGE is superb added to salads or sprinkled on fresh soups and tomatoes. In love, it is pleasant to inhale the aroma, which has an invigorating effect, and it also aids relaxation—but use just a little.

POPPIES are a dangerous subject! The field, poppy is the only poppy that can be used legally, and the seeds are safe to add to cooking, where they have a very uplifting effect. This poppy is also connected with pain relief in a less traumatic way than its relative, the opium poppy, which is addictive. For cooking, you should use only the seeds you can buy commercially. If you grow the corn poppy, use the red petals in potpourris.

BASIL is the most seductive of all Mediterranean herbs, cheering the spirit with its spicy aroma and calming the nerves when ingested. It is the most romantic herb for Italians, for whom it symbolizes deep love. Growing the plant is thought to be lucky, and nurturing it from seed is a signal to the divine spirit that you are ready for love.

The leaves of MYRTLE are used to flavor pork dishes and lamb. The connection with love is age-old and may be the result of its capacity to sweeten the breath.

MEADOWSWEET, sacred to the Druids, was used to flavor wines and to strew in the most important rooms: Gerard tells us it "makes the heart merrier." Use it in the bath to put your partner (and yourself, if the bathtub is big enough for two) in a loving mood.

CILANTRO, OR CORIANDER is an aromatic stimulant, and was added to love potions because of its aphrodisiac properties.

DIANTHUS (clove carnation) is a favorite ingredient in love potions and potpourris. This wonderful herb has a myriad uses: add the flowers to salads, wine, and cakes, and use in sauces, vinegars, and ales. It sweetens the breath, banishes headaches, quenches thirst, and brings on a gentle sweat. Need I say more?

With LAVENDER, we have saved the best till last. What does this herb not do? It is renowned in love for its capacity to alleviate nervous tension, ease digestive problems, and tranquilize after an overstimulating day. It also cheers the mind and kills bacteria and was added to soaps and baths for its obvious user-friendly properties. Indeed, for its antibacterial action alone it would be a friend to lovers. As an essential oil, it makes a wonderful salve for weary limbs, and can help ease skin disorders. Use it in cooking to rally flagging spirits!

USING THE MAGIC OF LOVE. You now have some of the tools with which to build a loving house. You should incorporate color, scent, herbs, and symbols wherever they please you. Choose those you like, that you can obtain readily, that are within your budget, and that perhaps have a certain significance for the love problem you want to solve.

The master spell in this chapter will provide you with the basic elements of a spell to attract (or strengthen) a love tie; if you want to get over a love relationship, look at chapter 6 instead.

Remember that you can choose whichever elements are relevant to *you*. Among the symbols presented in chapter 2, you should be able to find something pertinent to *your* lover, and the same is true for scents and herbs.

THERE ARE NO ABSOLUTES IN SPELL-MAKING—save for the warning not to become entangled with magic that is in any way detrimental to another being. Therefore, feel free to be creative.

DESIGN A SPELL YOU LIKE THE LOOK, FEEL AND SMELL OF—AND MAKE IT YOUR OWN.

MASTER SPELL: **TO ATTRACT LOVE.** This spell will work, with minor amendments, for a love who is as yet unknown, or for someone you are attracted to with (so far) no result, or for a person who has been flirting and playing with your feelings without becoming more serious.

YOU WILL NEED

1 yard of cherry-pink ribbon, and 2 other colors (see choices on page 41); a flask of red wine to which are added flowering herbs of your choice (pansy, borage, and dianthus are good for this, but use what you like); a dish of water to symbolize emotion; a cherry-pink taper, and 2 others (as before); clouds of incense burning to focus your thoughts (again, choose your favorite: benzoin or frankincense would be the usual choice, but you may prefer an essential oil simmering in a fragrancer); a lock of your hair.

MOON PHASE: *Full. Traditionally, this spell would be apt for Valentine's Day or the spring solstice—both of which occur near the time of the ash moon.*

Braid the three ribbons together, and tie them around your brow or waist. Strain your wine and sip a little in toast to the new era of love you are about to embark upon. Gaze up to the moon and ask a blessing of love; for the moon rules the realm of dreams. Ask that your dreams be transposed to the realm of earth—and stamp your foot softly on the ground to symbolize this. If you have anyone in particular in mind, say their name.

Say to the moon and starlight, *"Lovely lady's light that illumines the land, Seek out and bring my lover to hand, I offer my heart full of candor and pleasure, That soon may our lives meet in work or in leisure."* Meditate on the love you want.

Remember that the clearer and brighter your visualization, the more powerful your magic. Be sure you are not aiming your thoughts at someone who is tied to another.

Place the dish of water in a position where it can reflect the light—either from the candles you will light in a moment or from the moon. Now, turning to your candles and your incense or oil burner, light them with the words *"Love lights the way"* each time. If there is someone you are trying to entice, follow the phrase with their name as you light the candles.

Place the lock of hair in the center of the space created by the candles. Send the beam of candlelight into the air, higher and higher, until you can see it form a heart shape above you. Imagine the sound of laughter from your (known or unknown) lover. Breathe in the scent, and pass your lock of hair through it. Keep this for later and place it beside your bed.

The spell is complete when you feel you have sent your thought with sufficient strength. You can then untie the ribbon, and put it playfully in any number of spaces in your life: on your steering wheel, around your front-door knob, at your mailbox, in your underwear drawer, in your purse, around your dog's neck, even around your own! It would be nice tied around your pillow—to bring truth to your dreams.

After your tapers have burned down a little, extinguish them, and reserve for that special dinner you expect to share with your loved one.

VARIATIONS ON THE MASTER SPELL

IF YOU HAVE HAD A SUCCESSION OF FAILURES IN LOVE TO DATE, and there is no one special in your thoughts right now, take a photo of yourself from the past, tie the ribbons around it, and put a magnet on top of the picture, placing it then on the table where your candles are burning. On top of the photo/magnet, place a white rosebud. As you work the spell, imagine the bud gently opening to reveal a whole new you inside.

IF YOUR LOVE IS SOMEONE YOU HAVE HAD A BRIEF RELATIONSHIP WITH and you are trying to rekindle the spark one more time, take a piece of thorn (dead or alive) and wrap the ribbon around this instead of your waist, placing it in the center of the candles near the lock of hair. Put a small magnet on top of it to symbolize reversal of the current situation. REMEMBER: *This is not justified if the one you want is married to someone else!*

IF THE OBJECT OF YOUR AFFECTION IS A FOREIGNER, use a seashell in the spell: perhaps you could pass it through the candlelight and then put it into the dish of water, where it can remain for the duration of the spell-making. Afterward, put the ribbon with it (possibly in the shell) and cherish it as your key to unlocking love.

IF YOU WANT SOMEONE TO SHOW INTEREST, if there is any, by asking you to go out or just telephoning, take a red ribbon as well as the other three and wind it around your index finger. Think hard about the person getting in touch with you; then carry out the spell as above. When you have finished, unwrap the red ribbon from your finger and place it by the telephone, until you get that call.

IF YOU ARE DOING THIS SPELL TO ELICIT AN OFFER OF MARRIAGE, put a plain gold band on the table for the duration of the spell and strew petals (orange blossom, if available) on the ground around you. When you have finished with the ribbon, knot the ring into it and wear it around your neck for a week.

IF THE LOVE YOU HANKER FOR IS SOMEONE STILL GETTING OVER A PREVIOUS RELATIONSHIP (perhaps divorced, but still shy of relationships), sow a basil or pansy seed before you work the spell. When you have finished, tie the braided ribbons around the pot into which you have sown the seed, sending a healing love to the person in mind as you tie the bow. When the seedling sprouts, you will find the other party less emotionally timid: but nurture the young plant until things are out of danger.

IF YOU CANNOT CHOOSE BETWEEN TWO LOVES, perform this spell, but first write the names of the two candidates on two small pieces of paper (one on each) and light the candles with these tapers. As you do this, ask that the one who is right for you (if either) reveal themselves within the life of the present moon (i.e. a month). During that time, one or the other will seize your heart—or a new love will have arrived!

IF THE ONE YOU LOVE IS HOPELESSLY FLIRTING WITH YOUR FRIEND, and you think this is just an ego boost rather than a serious sign that things are not right between you, perform the master spell but place a sprig of myrtle (symbolizing honesty in love) on the table near the candles, and burn some grapefruit oil instead of the love oils. This will help you to deal with jealousy, in case the problem is not as serious as you feared.

IF YOU WANT TO INJECT PASSION INTO AN EXISTING RELATIONSHIP where, perhaps, the sexual element has lost its fizz, consult chapter 5 on passion.

IF YOU WANT TO EASE YOURSELF AWAY FROM A LOVE RELATIONSHIP THAT IS FINISHED, but refuses to let go completely, chapter 6 on disenchantment is the one for you.

☽

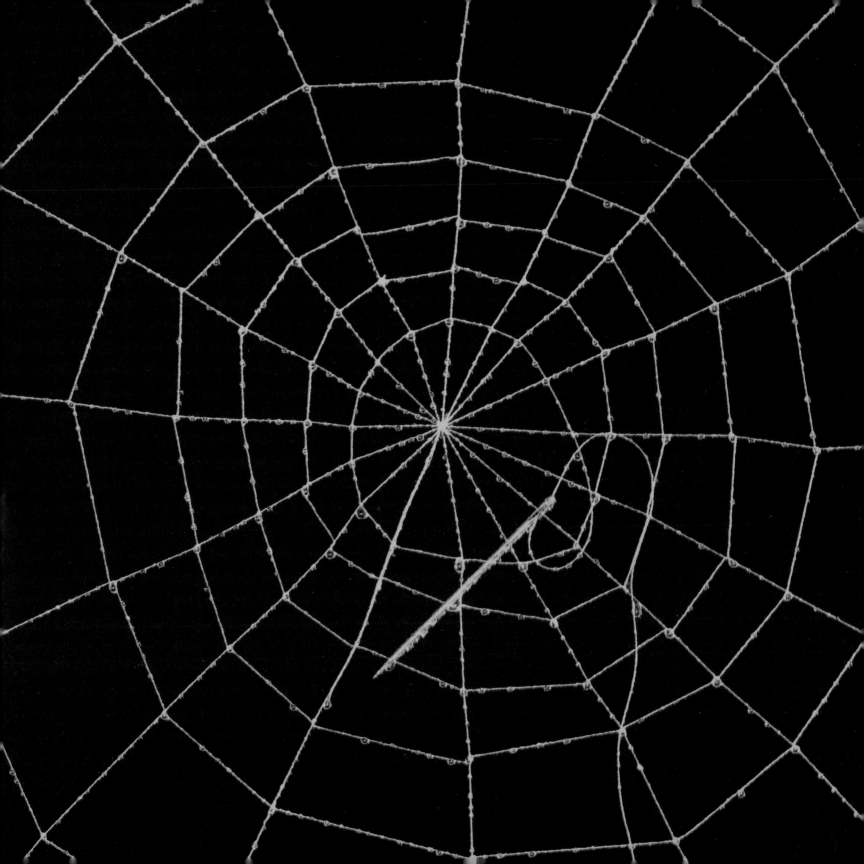

NOW EMBRACE THE SPRING EQUINOX, AS

OUR YEAR MOVES INTO THE MONTH OF THE ALDER MOON,

WHICH RUNS FROM MID-MARCH TO EARLY APRIL. AT THIS TIME WE

BEGIN TO LOOK AT THE YEAR'S WORK AND AT HOW TO EXECUTE OUR OWN DUTIES

EFFECTIVELY AND ENJOYABLY. THIS MOON GOVERNS ROUTINE BUSINESS AND HARD

WORK, AS OPPOSED TO THE LAUNCH OF ANYTHING REALLY SPECTACULAR, AND SPELLS

PERFORMED UNDER ITS SWAY WILL ENSURE A FAIR RESULT FROM THE ENTERPRISE.

WE ADDRESS THE ASPECT OF MAGIC IN PREPARATION FOR ALL KEY THINGS: DIGGING THE SOIL IN

4:WORK SPRING READY FOR SOWING SEEDS, PLANNING FOR SUCCESS

IN OUR EVERYDAY WORKING LIFE AND STUDY, KEEPING A

ROBUST BUSINESS THRIVING! THE MASTER SPELL IS FOR BRINGING HAPPINESS AT WORK, FOR WORK

DONE CHEERFULLY ALWAYS HAS BETTER RESULTS, AND WE DISCOVER HOW TO OVERCOME PROBLEMS

SUCH AS PERSONALITY CLASHES IN THE OFFICE OR WITH BUSINESS PARTNERS. THE ALDER MOON

REMINDS US THAT NOTHING IS GAINED WITHOUT SOME COMMITMENT AND PERSEVERANCE ON

OUR PART, AND THIS IS REFLECTED IN THE FIRST OF THE TWO SYMBOLS FOR THIS

CHAPTER. ONE IS "PATIENCE": THE TORTOISE, OR PERHAPS THE SNAIL, BOTH

LONG-HELD TALISMANS OF PATIENT WORK AND STEADY PROGRESS. THE

OTHER IS THE "GARDEN"—WHERE WHAT IS USEFUL MAY ALSO

BE BEAUTIFUL. PREPARE YOUR GROUND, AND

BLOSSOM FORTH!

ALDER MOON—MOON OF UTILITY AND SELF-GOVERNANCE. Colors: INDIGO, DEEP BLUE. Scents: CITRUS, BERGAMOT. Number: 4. The soundest preparation for success in any venture is to approach it with a determined, practical, and independent spirit. Magic looks at work as vital to the process of life's cycle: only after truly hard work is completed is a celebration, or vacation, felt in the very soles of the feet!

"Let us dig in our garden."
"CANDIDE"
VOLTAIRE

THE SPRING EQUINOX

The spring equinox falls on March 21. At this moment, as its name suggests, the earth is in perfect balance and day and night are of equal length. This was a powerful festival in times gone by. The sun—which was considered to be male—was in perfect harmony with the moon—which was female; the solstice is a divine symbol for the female receptivity of the earth preparing to take the (male) seed, and blossom forth. The first signs of spring flowers bursting with life are evidence that all is right in the divine world, and that the earth is blessed.

This month (approximately corresponding to our April) was given the Anglo-Saxon name of the goddess Oestra (or Eostre—Ostara in Latin); the corruption of this to Easter is self-evident. Certainly, the festival celebrates the return of the goddess from winter, and the burgeoning of spring with the promise of work ahead.

It is even probable that the hot cross bun of the Easter feast is derived from the female circle intersected by the male cross—the Celtic cross.

The Easter rabbit also stems from Pagan mythology, which recalls a rabbit or hare, messenger of the moon, honoring the goddess with a gift of the precious eggs that symbolized life by laying them at her feet, covered in a rainbow of colors. We re-enact the drama still.

Painting eggs, strewing rainbows of flowers, baking buns or breads and marking them with a cross, and especially growing hyacinths (which resemble wild bluebells) for your altar or table are ways of honoring the old magic within a modern context. Easter wine infused with a pinch of saffron and some blue flowers (try borage or violet) will put you in a wonderful loving mood—and honor the need for sowing the seeds of your future as well! Any work is achieved better through proper preparation. Flowers grow better when the rank weeds are removed and the hard-packed soil is combed and raked to a fine tilth. So it is with life. Magic can put us in the right frame of mind to undertake a task with dignity, stamina, and strength, while also adding a spark of playfulness to what might have been a dull chore. Add magical touches to all your workings, and watch the hours disappear more quickly while—magically—the successful outcome of your endeavor is also more assured.

To weave magic into your work requires a little creative thought. Performing magic spells in relation to work and gain will not bypass the need for your own contribution: it is not a formula for avoiding work and expecting the universe to provide. Instead, all the little rituals you introduce into your business life will be asking that work continue to find you— that you have plenty to do. An honest heart performing these rites will be hoping for ongoing opportunities, and luck in finding happy circumstances in a fulfilling working life.

THE COLORS OF WORK

An environment of blues will help you to think, study, and concentrate. Indigo is a powerful color for business, and of course blue is a primary color, just as work—be it mental or physical—is requisite to life. These colors embody the magic combination of clarity and stimulation, plus a reduction of tension. In other words, surrounding yourself with blues while you work will help you to focus your mind and find inner energy, and will neither sap your strength nor distract or stress you. Any office should have a strong blue element if it is to support the mental activity of the people who work therein. If painting the walls seems too radical, place a blue cushion on your chair, or hang a bluish picture near your desk. Or, wear blue clothes on a day when you simply have to get a lot done. Then, naturally, there are the magic things to do: tie a blue ribbon around your word processor when you close it down at night, so that it is there to greet you first thing the next day. Place a blue candle on your desk, and light it when you feel weary. Buy a blue coffee mug in a shade that inspires, and when you take a break, "breathe in" the color of the cup. If you really feel uninspired by the work you have to get through in order to meet a deadline, blue flowers in a vase—or, better still, a blue-flowered potted plant growing on your windowsill or desk—will really help to recharge your batteries at the moments of greatest apathy. And of course, you'll laugh when you think of it—especially if your boss has no idea why you have surrounded the latest project with potted blue hyacinths or African violets! Blue plates on the table, blue curtains, even a blue folder, will all help you get the job done more calmly.

THE SCENTS OF WORK

The citrus scents of orange, lemon, and grapefruit, plus bergamot, all have a purposeful effect on the mind and creative imagination. These oils are associated with energy, confidence, and positive performance, dispelling apathy and confusion, and piquing the brain into action. Perhaps for this reason, shower gels are now often spiked with citrus smells to get us going in the morning, and even men's grooming products favor bergamot to add a bracing quality to the unfolding day. Incorporating these fragrances into our work routine will make it easier to deal with the demands placed on us in a stressful society.

ORANGE may be the most important individual choice: neroli (orange blossom) is equally good here. If overwork and mental strain are a problem, this scent will neutralize the bad feelings that accompany such conditions.

LEMON is an antidote to feelings of sluggishness and tiredness, which are a common problem in work of every kind—even if you normally enjoy what you do.

GRAPEFRUIT helps to overcome frustrations (which might be caused by difficult relationships with others at work, or perhaps a job that never quite seems to get finished!) and can be useful if you are feeling apprehensive or indecisive.

Adding a touch of GINGER, BASIL, or ROSEMARY will help to counteract forgetfulness. Perhaps your work demands that you keep a thousand little things in your mind all the time—and in fact, these three scents are excellent in companionship with the other oils above if you have to study for an exam or absorb difficult schoolwork.

Assess the problems at the core of your working life, then choose any two or three of these oils to add to your blue colors, and push yourself back into peak performance. There is nothing wrong with burning these oils on your desk, or infusing your blue candle and lighting it for a few minutes several times a day. If others around you complain of the smell, keep a little blue herb pillow in your desk, sprinkle it with oil, and then inhale privately. You may set some tongues wagging—or you could set a trend!

PROBLEMS AT WORK. Sometimes, no matter how tolerant you try to be, someone just puts you on edge and makes you feel threatened. Maybe the person is more dominant than you, or seems to have a better relationship with someone in authority. The reverse is equally possible—that you have somehow engendered the wrath and jealousy of another! If you have to work with this person on a regular basis, you must deal with the difficulty or run the risk of making your job intolerable.

Jealousy and personality discord account for a huge amount of work misery, and sometimes result in a stand-off where one or the other of the parties feels compelled to resign. Don't let this happen, when there are witchy cures for the problem. What you must recognize, though, is that you do not want to make the other person more hostile (so revenge spells are definitely out!); you need instead to make them like you much better, until all animosity has been banished.

Bring a blue-flowered potted plant into the work domain, write both your name and that of your "adversary" on one small piece of paper, and push this gently into the soil around the plant. Tie the pot itself with ribbons—blue for perfected work, and either sunshine yellow (symbolizing a reversal of current circumstances) or olive green (symbolic of forgiveness). Place the plant somewhere everyone can enjoy it, and nurture it. Each time you water it, say something nice about the other person. Soon you will have them purring more contentedly around you!

LACK OF RECOGNITION

If your difficulty is one of being overlooked or taken for granted, you need to remedy this calmly. After a short time, the buildup of frustration becomes so immense that no amount of job satisfaction at other levels will counter it, and inevitably you will begin to feel that progress is almost impossible.

THE ANTIDOTE TO THIS PROBLEM CENTERS ON BEING ASSERTIVE: if you can show a more confident front, you will be neither stepped on nor patronized, and in addition you will be able to ask for what you really want without showing anger or anxiety. In short, you will feel a sense of control.

CHANGE YOUR PERFUME: mix a private blend of oils, and wear this for a few weeks. Always dilute your oils, and before you use one for the first time do a skin text, checking for a reaction after an hour or two. If you have no problem, then prepare for two weeks of scent-warfare. Keeping bergamot as the base, try 10 drops in 1 oz. of base oil (sweet almond is good), then add another 6 drops of jasmine, lime, carnation, or cyprus and 6 drops of neroli.

The night before you try this out, steep a blue ribbon in a little of the oil blend and place it under your pillow when you go to bed. Breathe in the scent, and feel the positivity creeping over you as you drift off to sleep. Visualize yourself being more bold and assertive in situations that would normally witness your retreat, and imagine yourself in control of events that you find frightening.

After a few days of this mental replenishment, and wearing your new fragrance, give your boss or unappreciative co-worker a new coffee mug or a plant, tied with the ribbon you have had under your pillow—but recharge the fragrance first. Within two weeks you will find you have made yourself much more visible—and much more appreciated!

DRESSING FOR INTERVIEWS

Whatever the glossy magazines tell you, a witch's advice for job and promotion interviews will always start with the wearing of blue underwear! My husband wears blue silk boxer shorts for important work occasions—and no one (I suppose) knows about this but me, but it gives him focus and self-discipline from the ground up!

With this as the starting point, individual taste will determine whether the outfit itself should be smart or casual, a skirt or pants, velveteen or linen. Try to arrange the meeting for a new moon, and begin by bathing (or showering) with those citrus scents. Don't wear any designer fragrance, but do put on some of the diluted citrus oils, or dab a little undiluted onto your watch strap, purse, belt, or briefcase—the person talking to you will be just as alert as you!

When you get home, give a libation (a small drink) of ale or wine to your favorite tree in the park or in your yard. Traditionally this would have been an alder tree, but any tree will suffice as long as you explain that you are hoping for strong growth to come from the seed you have just planted at your interview. *This has always been lucky for those I know.*

STARTING A BUSINESS

If you are trying to launch a concern of your own—be it a sandwich shop, a design business, a career as a pop star, a caregiving agency, or perhaps a career as a writer—till the soil

first! Wait for a new moon before "going public" or signing any contracts; choose a name that has the letter "D," "M" OR "V" in it to signify an inclination to work hard—a letter for material success ("H," "Q" or "Z") will also be a huge help.

The next step is to get your color scheme right: remember to put blue somewhere to the fore, and couple this with any color that symbolizes the kind of work you do (see notes on color in each chapter). Tie ribbons and balloons everywhere to get attention and put energy into the new operation; regularly burn candles infused with the scents described on page 54 in the window or near the phone. And definitely put plants of glowing good health all around you—especially those with blue flowers.

Last, write the name of your new business on a small piece of paper, and on the full moon after you have launched take it to some running water. Let it go with the blessing that your new working life will be like a river of depth, feeling, gentle power, and the ability to adapt to any circumstances, and watch it sail forth into the world. Be confident, and you will not fail.

KICK-STARTING A SLUGGISH BUSINESS

The first cure for a business (yours or anyone else's) that is making slow progress is to inject energy into it everywhere. This is a fun project, and you should draw everyone into it!

Write the name of the suffering business on paper and place it under a red candle (for a new start) and a blue candle, either in the office or in your home. Tie a white ribbon around the base of each one, to add more power via white light. Burn the candles for an hour or two each day, and imagine light moving around the business environment, gaining energy and attracting interest from lots of people. Put a potted plant (blue, of course!) in a prominent spot in the workplace, and push the name that has been under your candles into the soil. Tie the

ribbon around the plant. Meanwhile, tie a red ribbon around
the telephone at work: this encourages more calls. Sprinkle a few
drops of citrus oil near the threshold of the workplace, to put
visitors in a zappy, responsive state of mind. Mark the place in
the telephone book where the office number appears with a card
dotted with a little of the oil, and put a blue ribbon in there too.

Finally, send thriving plants (oddly enough, potted
coriander tied with blue ribbon is a good choice here) all over
the place to attract more activity into the business: give them
to friends and family, and offer them to acquaintances.
Distributing growing plants in this way will send out signals of
"good grace" concerning the business.

Continued Success

If yours is the happy predicament of being really fortunate and
fulfilled in your choice and situation of work, and you merely
wish to keep it that way ad infinitum, yours is the simplest magic
to perform, but you will nevertheless be pleased with the
result. Many people take success for granted—as their right—
and forget to show grace when they are favored.

Take a silver coin and place it in the palm of your hand,
facing the sunlight, so that it glints a little in the light. Say
thanks many times over for the flow of work and funds that has
come your way, then say the name of your business or the place
where you work, four times out loud. Wrap the coin in blue
cloth or ribbon, and place it somewhere over the door in your
office, or tape it to the desk at which you work. Touch it every
so often with a brief word of thanks.

HONORS AT SCHOOL OR COLLEGE

Absorb every bit of the advice given so far in this chapter in one way or another into your life as a student. Put a potted plant with beautiful blue flowers on your new teacher's desk each year; cover boring textbooks with indigo (and silver) paper; keep a ribbon impregnated with the citrus scents in your pencil case, and breathe it in whenever you are having a humdrum day; and try to present really important work in a blue-bordered folder.

Before your first day at a new institution, plant a seedling of a blue, fragrant flower (sweet peas are always my favorite) and write your own name and that of the new college, teacher, or whatever on a piece of paper pushed gently into the pot. On really dull days (weather- or subject-wise), ask your teacher or professor if you can hang a balloon, place a vase of flowers, or scent the room with a burner to keep everyone attentive: they probably won't mind a bit. My daughter has a bookmark saturated with lime and lemon which she places in her math books when required: this is her least favorite subject, and the scents help her to knuckle down to the work at hand.

Although much work is arduous duty, it is always completed more quickly and satisfactorily if you bring a sparkle to it. I first fell in love with Schubert's *"Death and the Maiden"* while I was scrubbing my kitchen floor—for it literally transported me above the humdrum task. Forever after, scrubbing the floor has been the moment to discover new music, and lose myself in the task.

DOMESTIC WORK

Never let it be thought that bringing up a family is unrecognized by this witch for the truly hard work that it is. I think raising a family and managing a home (of whatever size) well is the hardest job of all—especially if it is combined with part-time work, study, or community responsibility. There is a special magic to help temper the demands of a busy home—and again, it should also put a little more fun into routine work.

Think over the daily run of chores, and decide what objects can receive the playful blue ribbon or the drops of oil. Visitors to my house will often see ribbons tied to refrigerator doors, irons, bottles of dishwashing detergent, washing baskets, and brooms. All these make me laugh when I have to settle down to the job required with each item. There is also a huge blue ribbon tied to the chair I sit on when writing. Without this I might experience energy block—especially when I have essays, letters, chapters of books, and a baby vying for my time. Think blue ribbons everywhere!

The next step is to decorate the windowsill of the room in which you work most with plants that will thrive in that environment. My desk boasts a potted lemon tree—combining two ideas, as it were—and basil, coriander, and African violets jostle together on the windowsill. I also have a blue hydrangea on the windowsill in my bedroom—which is where I often read, study, and perform magic.

Lastly, the element that governs work is "earth"—so work with some as often as you can. Plant a seedling every so often, or cultivate a windowbox, if a full garden is out of the question. Quite simply, dirtying your hands is good for all business!

☾

MASTER SPELL: **FOR HAPPINESS IN WORK.** This spell is based on the simple concept that the happier we are in what we do, the more successful we will be at it. It also safeguards contentment in all the aspects of our work: socially, financially, and in terms of challenge. You will not be taken for granted by anyone.

YOU WILL NEED
1 yard each of blue and gold cord, of the same texture; a piece of paper; an emblem of your work; golden yellow sunflowers (symbolizing both material success and happiness of spirit); blue flowers, such as violets, hyacinths, hydrangeas, lavender, or anything else available in season; 1 golden and 1 blue taper.

MOON PHASE: *Anytime from new through to full.*

Perform this spell when you are feeling happy and positive. Make a circle in the middle of your busiest room by placing the blue and gold cords in semicircles opposite each other, so that they join, thereby making a complete circle of two different colors. Write your name on the paper, place it in the middle, and put near it an emblem of the work you do—make it a pen if you write a lot, a book if you study or teach, a domestic item if you tend the house, something edible if you cook, paint or fabric if you're creative, or anything else that readily springs to mind that is symbolic of your professional life. Now, make an arrangement of all the flowers and put them in the center of the circle as well. Last of all, light the candles and place them in the circle.

Walk once around the circle, asking for security and pleasure in your working life; ask that you contribute utility, that your contribution be positive, and that you be valued fairly for it. Look out at the sky, and think of the busy universe; of the world stirring around you; of all the balanced activity, refined by thousands of years of interconnection. See yourself in the midst of this web.

Lift the flowers out of the circle, kiss them, and place them on a central table; the next day, transfer them to the place where you work. Take your cords and make a big bow from them, tying them anywhere that makes you smile (a wastebasket is fun!). The candles need only burn for about an hour—thereafter, light them from time to time to ask for blessings on your work.

Remember to grow blue flowers in a pot at work, and if you like, tie the cords together around the big pot. YOUR WORK LIFE WILL BLOSSOM.

THE
LESSON IN THIS CHAPTER IS BOUND TO THE
WILLOW MOON, KNOWN AS THE WITCHES' MOON, WHICH
RULES THE PERIOD FROM MID-APRIL TO EARLY MAY. IT IS NOW TIME TO
EXPLORE THE CRUCIAL ASPECT OF SELF-EMPOWERMENT, WHICH HAS SIGNIFICANT
IMPACT ON EVERY AREA OF LIFE. SYMBOLS FOR PERSONAL STRENGTH AND TALISMANS
FOR PERSONAL FULFILLMENT ARE USED HERE. THE MASTER SPELL IS ONE TO "ENCHANT"—
THAT IS, TO WIN ANYONE OVER COMPLETELY TO YOUR POINT OF VIEW! THIS INCLUDES LOVE,
BUSINESS, AND SOCIAL FUNCTIONS, BUT BEING "ENCHANTED" IS ALSO CONCERNED WITH THE

5:ENCHANTMENT

PASSIONS, AND THIS
CHAPTER SHOWS HOW
TO ADD PASSION TO YOUR LIFE AND HOW TO KEEP UP A MAGICAL DANCE, ENCHANTING THE SENSES
WITH SENSUALITY. THIS IS THE MOMENT TO LEARN HOW TO DISCOVER YOUR PERSONAL CHARISMA—
AND, AS SUCH, IS THE MOST IMPORTANT PHASE FOR THE SELF. THE SABBAT, OR FEAST DAY, THAT
FALLS IN THIS PERIOD IS THE BEST KNOWN OF ALL—MAY DAY, OR BELTANE. THE "LUSTY
MONTH OF MAY" WAS ALWAYS CONNECTED WITH SPECIAL FERTILITY RITES AND THE
PASSAGE FROM VIRGINAL SPRING TO VOLUPTUOUS LATE SPRING'S FULL-BODIED
WARMTH. THUS, THE MAYPOLE FEATURES STRONGLY HERE, AND THE
RIBBONS AND THEIR COLOR SIGNIFICANCE ARE EXPLAINED, SO
THE CUSTOM OF A MAYPOLE DANCE MAY YET
BE REVIVED.

WILLOW MOON—MOON OF ENCHANTMENT. Colors: PURPLE, WISTERIA, LAVENDER. Scents: LAVENDER, SANDALWOOD, BENZOIN. Number: 5. The language of love and the passions draws heavily on magic. We are "charmed" by someone initially, "enchanted" perhaps; and the first flush of deeper love certainly feels like a spell that is working in spite of logic or the banal demands of our normal lives.

> "A little still she strove, and much repented,
> And whispering 'I will ne'er consent'—consented."
> FROM CANTO I, "DON JUAN"
> LORD BYRON

The feeling of falling in love lifts us above the humdrum; everything gray takes on a sunnier face. This is possibly because our senses are, in a way, "intoxicated"; and if we can recapture that for ourselves, and promote it in others, our lives can be transposed from pastels to bright colors at will.

ENCHANTMENT HAS A PLACE IN EVERY ASPECT OF OUR LIVES. We can grow an "enchanted" garden, luring creatures and eliciting beauty from it on a paradisical scale (even in a few square yards). We can enchant in our working lives, to keep others happy and cooperative, and business ticking over quietly. We can enchant family and friends with simple measures that will add depth and color to their lives. We can enchant our lovers to add dimension, beauty, and durability to the relationship.

What we cannot do is enchant anyone for the purpose of gaining power "over" them—by which I mean holding them "in thrall." Magic must always be an invitation to greater richness, a bolder tapestry of life: it cannot be a license to

manipulate others for your gain. This would, quite simply, be an abuse of trust. Never convince yourself that it is fair to curtail someone else's life in order to enhance your own: getting someone fired in order to take their job, or spreading gossip to undermine another's confidence for your own gain, is not the work of a white witch—and is a recipe for disaster.

That said, we will examine the ways in which we can use enchantment to improve our lot. And for this, we need the willow tree and the willow moon. It is the tree sacred to witches, and some will even say that they would rather not have it in the house, because of its immense power and, of course, its association with "weeping." But it is this very association with human feeling that gives it that special something in white magic.

THE NATURE OF WILLOW
Willow grows along riverbanks, ditches, waterways, fens, and other marshy land where water is abundant. Water is the element that governs the emotions, so this places willow symbolically in the realm of "feeling," as it understands and incorporates that medium of emotion into its system. Because of its sensitivity to water, it is one of the chief trees used in water divination, and this alone was enough to place it high in the esteem of the Druids and Celts. In fact, the willow has been revered for

centuries by many cultures for its bark, which contains salicylic acid—the basis of aspirin. Drinking willow bark tea was a cure for fevers; the leaves as well as the bark have long been used to treat pain, headache, inflammations, even rheumatism and arthritis. For its aspirin-like uses, the tree was always one of the favorite medicinal herbs used by the healers of ancient people—witches being no exception.

Making a knot of willow harnesses its strength and proclaims the spell-maker a witch of the blood. Willow is there for your use, and for me symbolizes a maiden with tresses reaching all the way to the earth, incorporating the waters of time—and thus wisdom—in its sap. Learn to respect the willow's power: but do not fear it. Think of this as an electric current, and handle it wisely.

A true witch, then, will want a willow tree growing in their garden, or in a pot on their roof or balcony. Get advice from a garden centre or good nursery, choose a large enough pot, water the plant well, and it will love you like a human friend.

The Willow Knot

This is a step toward enchantment. Bend a small, soft, pliable piece of just-green willow gently into a knot like a figure eight, and as you do this make a little prayer to honor the goddess (which can simply mean that you will consider the patterns and needs of Mother Earth). Think of yourself as part of the chain of other wise exponents of the craft going before you, and as you weave your knot with your prayer, think loving thoughts to all those who cross your mind – including difficult landladies and sharp-tongued in-laws! In other words, weave a spell of magical enchantment as you tie your little knot. Think musical, happy thoughts: see yourself, like Orpheus in the Greek legend, taming savage entities with the enchanting sound. This knot will find its way into our master spell and variations, but you can also use

it in "everyday" magic by placing it among the daily tools of your profession, in your pocket as you meet people, in your home for protection, or even under the tablecloth if you have an important dinner engagement. It gives you bewitching power, good humor, wisdom, and grace—and *these are the elements of self-empowerment on a major scale.*

May Day

MAY DAY (Beltane) is the most important Wicca feast of the year, next to Samhain (Halloween). The latter was the New Year (and ushering-in of the winter); this is the start of the summer year, and the celebration of the most fertile, prosperous, optimistic moment in the calendar. The name seems to derive from the Scottish sun deity, Bel, or the Celtic god of fire and reflects the importance of the warmer months (then and now). It is also thought that the word derives from that for a "balefire"—the bonfire that was always lit on May Day eve (April 30).

Get up at dawn on May Day and make strong magic for a powerful year. It was traditional to gather may (hawthorn) flowers—despite the legend that bringing them into the house risked fairies' coming in too!—as making a wish on the dew-bedecked flowers was a guarantee of its fruition.

The May Queen is an incarnation on earth of the full-blown spring goddess, and her Italian cousin is Flora, bringer of spring flowers and symbol of full summer fertility and love. Even the Phrygian sibyl was an ancestress of the spring goddess—her particular festival being "hilaria," which was a romp of sensuality!

May is thus associated with love of the flirtatious, extra-marital kind. This is not the divine marriage, but the moment of the senses overflowing with ripeness. Thus, to go "a-maying" was a euphemism for gathering may flowers from the hawthorn and tasting the pleasures of illicit love—a licentiousness almost condoned by custom! The flowers were often beribboned, and young suitors would hang their bunch at the door of the girl they liked: far wilder and more unbridled than Valentine's Day!

   If you want to celebrate Beltane, go a-maying to your local flower-seller, or pick wildflowers in hedges or on wasteland. Get some friends to resurrect the maypole with you: it is, after all, the great symbol of May lust, love, and liberation! You need a pole taken from either the may tree or birch; in some climates, pine has been used. In any event, your pole must be stripped of its greenery, which now makes it resemble a great phallic symbol, and should be carried by a party of revelers to the spot where it will be raised. It is then festooned with flowers and herbs, and ribbons—red (for the god), white (for the goddess), and green (for verdancy and fertility)—should be fixed to the top; if other colors are added, blue or purple is usually the next choice. With friends, you could create a wonderful May feast, bringing picnic foods decorated with flowers and herbage, and dancing the intricate "May dance" around the pole, weaving the ribbons into an elaborate pattern as you go. It is not difficult to see the origin of a fertility rite here: the phallic pole is inserted into the female, receptive earth, feet drum out a sensual stimulus, and the flowers represent a kind of expectation of blossoming life.

   This is accompanied by a chant that raises the power of the earth and draws down blessings on the dancers. Pin a circlet of birch leaves or a willow knot, or both, to your clothing, and wish your heart away. Remember that you are beginning to gain the power to enchant—so use your new strength kindly.

THE SCENTS OF ENCHANTMENT. Scent can bewitch at a stroke. Our brains are especially responsive to scents that arouse our passions because, at the most basic level, it is this that ensures the continued reproduction of the species. Some scents make us feel sexually aroused instantly, others entice our interest, and still others make us feel good in the company of the people with whom we share the scent. We must therefore learn to use the right one at the right time!

The scents to make another passionate, and that are thus the right choice for sensuality shared with another, are expensive: but there really is no substitute for quality.

TUBEROSE is the most wonderful scent. It is difficult to come by, and you may have to settle for a tuberose-based perfume, or at best a perfume oil (this is not pure oil, but carries the perfume of the flower). I buy tuberose in Paris; it is forbiddingly expensive, but a little goes a very long way. I save it for very special occasions when nothing else will quite do. A tiny drop will counteract irritability and emotional conflict; it also arouses sensuality, motivates, invites spontaneity, and can even transform an introverted person into a more outgoing personality. When you consider that all these effects will be felt by both the wearer of the oil or perfume and those who smell it, you can see its true potential. My advice would definitely be that it is worth a trip to Paris!

JASMINE is related to tuberose, and some of the effects are similar. It has the power to make you feel almost hypnotized: sexual, confident, inspired, near-euphoric. It also counters some of the negative traits that hinder passion, such as anxiety, poor self-esteem, jealousy, guilt, and tension. It can even dispose of feelings of frigidity, which explains its popularity as an aphrodisiac scent in the East. Again, my advice is that it is well worth its high price tag.

GARDENIA oil has almost all the properties of the above. To ensure a supply, grow pots of gardenias. If you have a romantic dinner planned and want a straight ticket to the boudoir without even getting to the dessert, place a flowering plant squarely in the middle of the table. You're halfway there. Put another cut flower just by your bed. Voilà! If you are lucky enough to find the perfume oil, or even the essential oil, you will discover it to be a wonderful scent to help anyone overcome feelings of fear and depression about past failures in bed or in relationships. It is also a good oil for those who have previously suffered violence in a sexual or an emotional climate.

YLANG-YLANG has a gigantic reputation as an aphrodisiac and is the oil most closely synonymous with sensual warmth and joyfulness. It generates a feeling of self-confidence, awakens those who are excessively fatigued, and also combats chronic shyness. What more could you possibly ask for?

LAVENDER adds compassion and gentleness to the mix. Instead of inflaming the passions, it excites more gently, though it does rejuvenate and comfort after a difficult day. Lavender is marvelous to use in tandem with other oils if there is an element of forgiveness, or tentativeness, to counteract. It is also wonderful just to strew the fresh herb (grow it for this purpose alone) around your bed. It looks great on crisp white linen, and after lifting you to dizzy, sensual heights, it will relax you for a perfect sleep in the afterglow of passion. Perhaps this is the secret of happy life in southern France?

SO, HOW SHOULD YOU INCORPORATE THESE SCENTS INTO YOUR SORCERY OF PASSION? Set the mood for intimate dinners by dispersing the scent via a burner; bathe in your own personal mixture of these scents (or keep one pure); scent the sheets; spray some on the lightbulb; infuse the candles with a little fragrance; dab some on your pulse points, properly diluted or dilute the scents in water (4 drops essential oil to 10 fl. oz. water) in an atomizer and, last but not least, spray a little on your hair or into your car or briefcase. This is pheromone manipulation of the most serious kind.

THE COLORS OF ENCHANTMENT

LAVENDER appears in the color chart as well as on the olfactory shortlist: the purples are the colors of power and passion. It is difficult to refuse a person who is in control of purple, and this is a point to remember. If you cannot feel strong in purple, and sense instead that it is wearing you, tone it down to lavender or wisteria.

Tips for a successful social function, speech, or party would be to spread the color purple profusely around the room, disperse the scents listed on page 67, and tie a great knot of willow over the threshold like mistletoe. I like purple balloons into which a few drops of scent have been placed. When they burst (and they always do after a while), a shower of joy breaks into the room and rains sunshine on the proceedings.

Flowers chosen in these hues are as apt for the boardroom as the bedroom; ribbons should find a place, too. If you tie silverware for an executive lunch with purple ribbon, everyone will wait to hear from you. You will also gain a reputation for an interesting design style!

THE SYMBOLS OF ENCHANTMENT

- The strongest visual encouragement for someone to listen to you, and attend to all you say and do, is the WILLOW KNOT. Wear it around your neck or pinned to a coat. You will receive some interesting inquiries about it before the day is over!

- The other main symbols for enchanting are a SPIDER'S WEB (which you might get made into jewelry), and large MOONSTONES—which resemble the color, size, and density of the willow moon. Charge their power first from the moon's rays and wear them with a special prayer in mind. Wish on them with great belief and positivity. Never doubt.

- The ACORN and OAK LEAF, are other symbols of confidence and the power to enchant. Carry one with a sense that you have a secret weapon against all negativity.

- Lastly, a KEY, tied with a small scrap of purple ribbon, is a powerful talisman indeed with which to enchant a person and wish that they will hear every word you say, hanging on each one. Place the key on a beautiful silver key ring, charged with the moon's light. This will make a very personal but powerful attractor of magical thought and translator of your own vibration.

ENCHANTMENT IN EVERYDAY LIFE

If you wish to work a little enchantment daily, gently turn up the volume of passion in your relationship, or simply make others in your home feel loved, go a little crazy with purple or lavender ribbons and fragrance in odd places.

Tie back your bed curtains with purple ribbons; tie purple ribbons around the silverware you place at dinner; trail a purple ribbon (and candles alongside) from your living room to your bed; and tie a purple (or possibly red) ribbon around some intimate part of your body. Hang lavender-stuffed slippers above your bed, then wear the shoes the next day for bewitching power: people will fall at your feet!

If you simply want to keep your dwelling purified and tease visitors about the emblematic significance of it, you could cut a "wand" (no more than 15–20 in. long) from a birch tree on a full moon, tie a beautiful bow of flame-red around it, and place it above a mantelpiece, on a bookshelf, or anywhere else in your home that pleases you.

MASTER SPELL: **TO ENCHANT AND GAIN SELF-EMPOWERMENT.** This spell is requisite to any really important task you have to fulfill concerning your own life. It is relevant (possibly in tandem with a particular love spell) to sallying forth to meet a long-lost lover, or following an argument; it is beneficent when you are applying for a job, or taking an exam; it is imperative if you have to win someone over to your way of thinking. DO NOT ABUSE IT ....

YOU WILL NEED
A sprig of willow, tied into a simple knot; 5 candles in a purple (tending to wisteria) hue; any of the oils described in this chapter, plus peony, wisteria, or carnation perfume oil; 1/2 yard of purple ribbon; purple underwear—bought specially for this occasion!

MOON PHASE: *Waxing.*

The night before your important appointment, tie the willow sprig gently into a simple knot and place it by your bedside. Place your right hand through the knot (or, if you have only a small piece, place your index finger into it) and "breathe in" the colors and scent of the willow. From your toes upward, imagine the little pliable twig bringing you energy, hope, and confidence.

Next morning, before your appointment, light the candles and place them next to the willow, then sprinkle a few drops of the oil on the willow knot itself. Tie the ribbon loosely around one of the candles, and make a very calm direction:

"All that follows from this day, Will rest within my power, Though magic, such, is pure child's play, My good grace shall not sour."

Now envision, very simply, a brief picture of the resolution you desire: someone shaking your hand to conclude the business, or a love holding you with warmth and renewed passion, or an exam passing off without difficulty, and so on. Stand up and bow slightly to the burning candles, then dress—beginning with the special undergarments, which you should first sprinkle with the passion oils described on page 67.

As you put on your clothes, look at the candles and see the success you want attending you: imagine everything will go your way, and promise not to abuse this. Finally, blow out the candles, untie the ribbon, and tie it instead around your stockinged thigh (or wrist, if you prefer), then put a dab of the oil on your pulse points. Pop the willow knot—the most important talisman—into a pocket or your purse, and quietly repeat the words above as you do so. The outcome of your event should now be everything you could wish for. NO ONE CAN REFUSE YOU TODAY!

VARIATIONS ON THE MASTER SPELL

IF YOU ARE GOING TO MAKE A TELEVISION
APPEARANCE, or give a speech, or perhaps get married today,
use this variation to make sure everything goes off well. In
tandem with the master spell, burn seven candles of the colors of
the rainbow with the five purple ones, and add seven matching
ribbons, each 1/2 yard long, to the purple ribbon. Place these
colored ribbons anywhere you like, to make them either visible
or not (as you prefer): tie them into your hair in tiny little bows,
or tie them all around your ankle or wrist, or place a rainbow
around your thigh, and you will bring a rainbow of positivity
and empowerment to your special day.

IF YOU WANT TO ATTEND AN AUCTION for a
house and make sure you get it, burn one white
candle with the five purple ones: white is the
color of home and hearth.

IF YOUR EMPOWERMENT CONCERNS
REVERSING A DIFFICULT LOVE AFFAIR,
in which until now your lover has had power over you, burn a
rose-pink candle with the other five, sprinkle rose oil on your
underwear, and jump over a broom—which you should place at
the threshold—as you leave the house.

)

IF THE SPELL IS SPECIFIC TO TAKING AN EXAM, braid a yellow ribbon and a brick-colored ribbon (the colors of material stability and analysis) with the purple, then continue with the master spell; substitute lavender oil for the peony, wisteria, or carnation oils to get your brain working well.

IF YOU ARE ASKING FOR A BANK LOAN, try wearing some bronze-based jewelry while you perform the spell, and add three candles in bronze or sunshine yellow (for money) to the five purple ones; then carry on.

IF YOU ARE HOPING TO PERSUADE AN EMPLOYER TO PROMOTE YOU, wear silver jewelry and burn four silver candles in addition to the purple ones, but dab them first with jasmine or melissa oil. When you go into your meeting, take your employer one beautiful single-stemmed flower in a purplish color, and make sure it is scented—stock is ideal, or better still, a purple-red rose.

IF YOU ARE TAKING A PET TO A SHOW, or a horse to a trial, and you want it to perform well, find a sprig of holly (available all year, without the berries!) and place it by the candles. Follow the master spell, and when you have untied the ribbon, tie it first around your wrist, then put it around the animal's neck, or under the horse's saddle. Submission will follow!

IF YOU HAVE A COURT APPEARANCE, and you want to come out well and be heard without feeling timorous, perform the whole master spell, then tie a black and a white ribbon, 1/2 yard each in length, around your wrist or thigh—braid all three together if you like. This will boost your sense of mastery and help you to feel in control.

There

comes a moment when you must turn

off feelings that are not desired. This need is

symbolized in the hawthorn moon—the moon of hindrance,

which covers the period mid-May to early June—and this chapter

concerns spells to disenchant, which are a vital part of magic. If someone

is being impossibly persistent about something you really don't wish to do, this

is where to look for help. It has relevance for those who believe (or know) that

they are attracting attention from an undesirable quarter—such as a past lover,

6:DISENCHANTMENT

a friend's partner, a boss, or someone else trying to abuse a position of authority. It may

equally be that you are feeling an attraction yourself to someone ill-advised (such as

any of the above), and it would be well to look to appropriate magical ways of

nipping unwise attractions in the bud. The moon of hindrance also takes care

of unwelcome intruders: perform these magical rites to minimize the

threat of unwanted guests in your home (even cats and dogs!) or

to put up a magical barrier between your serenity and the

outside world. The master spell is designed to rid

you of a past love affair or an unwanted

admirer.

HAWTHORN MOON—MOON OF DISENCHANTMENT. Colors: ROSE-PINK, WHITISH-PINK. Scents: CAMPHOR, MINT, PINE, PEPPER. Number: 6. There is a double nuance to the beautiful hawthorn tree. One face it wears is that of the smiling, beguiling may flower that we discovered in chapter 5; as such, it understands well the subjects of love, flirtation, and unruly passion. Its other face, however, is of the greater concern to us here: for hawthorn is the first choice, in England, for creating an impenetrable barrier between farm fields, or constructing a castle wall of protection around the family home. If you wish to keep anything out, choose thorn!

"And on a day we meet to walk the line,
   And set the wall between us once again."
"MENDING WALL"
ROBERT FROST

In a sense, it is this compassionate ambivalence that makes hawthorn the right choice for working magic that requires an emotional understanding of feeling and attraction, while realizing that, for whatever reason, it should be curtailed. This moon and this tree wish no harm on the other party—as with all white magic. If you are going to ask that someone to respect your boundaries, you must do so with charm, grace, and sensitivity. Hence, the flowering thorn: it is relevant and indeed significant that the tree flowers throughout the whole period of the hawthorn moon. Thus, tread softly on another's dreams! Soften your thorny words of protection with flowers of friendship, and lovingly ask that the other party desist! Most of the time you will prefer to enchant people—THE HAWTHORN IS FOR USE ONLY WHEN THIS HAS GOTTEN OUT OF HAND!

THE HAWTHORN KNOT

As with the enchanter's knot made of willow in chapter 5, this is a talisman you will need to keep with you if you are waging a little war of attrition with a persistent suitor; it can also be used in any situation where you are trying to disenchant someone. Pick a little piece of hawthorn branch (take care of your fingers!) on a waxing moon; you will use it on a waning moon in spell-making.

Work at night, and ask that your thorn knot protect you from unwelcome attentions, unsolicited advances, or unwise thoughts on your own part toward anyone else. Using gloves, if necessary, weave your thorn into a beautiful figure eight knot. The "eight" protects from an infinite number of possibilities; but if you cannot work an eight knot, make a simple loop (like a ring) which will keep for eternity. As you knot, say, *"I wish no other being harm, but wish myself safe and secure in the loop of my own identity."* Place the knot somewhere safe, such as inside a lidded box. You want to be able to take the knot out at will and choose when to use it, rather than have it work as a constant repellant.

THE SCENTS OF RESTRAINT. If you need to restrain the thoughts and actions of another, or if you need to exercise self-restraint, the scent must be one of abruptness, a discouraging fragrance—one that will brace you or your adversary and wake you up to the messages that are being given.

MINT is the place to start: in fact, research indicates that mint works as a deterrent to animals in the garden, helps to mollify wild dogs, and signals the brain to think intelligently rather than emotionally. Many mixtures based on mint are worthy of a place in the weaponry of refusing love.

BLACK PEPPER also wakes a suitor out of reverie and asks that they attend to the words actually being spoken—not those they would like to imagine were forthcoming. Thus, for instance, if you were to have dinner with someone you really wanted to deter from making advances, a mixture of black pepper and mint spritzed onto your wrist and pulse points would be quite a turn-off.

PINE has a strongly disinfectant smell, and is bracing rather than sensual. This is a good choice if you are experiencing harassment at work: you will be equated with the cleaner, and will not appear nearly so desirable!

CAMPHOR is famous for its capacity to deter anything living. It is sometimes hard to find camphor oil itself, but you can use camphor-based ointments, or burn the leaves from a camphor laurel tree to release the scent, or at worst use mothballs, which are based on camphor. Camphorated oil may be available from your pharmacy, as it is used as a decongestant.

Use any of these oils as inhalants from which to meditate dissuasive thoughts to the party causing you problems.

Sit in the center of a ring of pinkish-white light, cast by six pink candles and six white, placed alternately, and envision your subject. Place a heavy beam of light between you—dividing rather than connecting you. Scent that beam with the fragrances around you: imagine a great peppermint stick of pink and white light creating a "wall" between you. Or draw a line of pepper in white light; or surround the other person in a glow of warm light to wish them well, but scent that light with clouds of camphor.

If you understand that the colors you use are made up of loving shades, you will realize how important compassion is. It is almost like saying, *"If you love me, let me go."* Asking someone to release you in a hostile manner is, psychologically, more like an invitation to their ego to prove that they can overcome your lack of feeling. Asking that someone respect your wishes, while remaining gracious, is harder to deny. Of course, along with that politeness there is the scent of refusal. YOU MUST ENVISION THE EFFECT VERY POWERFULLY, FOR ONLY THEN WILL YOUR BARRIER BE RESPECTED.

HONORING THE MAY THORN

There is a strange duality about the hawthorn, or may tree. Because the honoring of the god and goddess in Pagan mythology occurred in May, when the tree was at full stretch, blossoming its heart out, the hawthorn came to be seen as synonymous with blessings from the gods. Then, too, the month of May was connected with revels and witchcraft, and the tree was said to be enchanted, so that cutting boughs of hawthorn was a possible way of letting fairy folk into the house.

The may tree was a visual symbol of beauty and enchantment; its thorn was a symbol of obstruction. At the end of the May festival, the god and goddess were "killed off" as part of the ritual of progress that would develop over the continuing summer—eventually to lead to a renewed life cycle the following year. For this reason, the hawthorn was associated with hope and fertility, but was also an omen of death; the tree is both lucky and unlucky. It is this paradox that encompasses the hawthorn tree/moon as one of love and of hindrance. Always remember this dichotomy when you are working magic to repel someone. There must be love, and positivity, combined with your dissuasive intention.

To protect yourself from misplaced affection, include thorn leaves in your salads, or put them in your sandwiches for work. The tree was actually known as "bread-and-cheese" because the leaves taste so good used in this way—and you will know the consumption of the plant also has a witchy significance! If a co-worker is becoming distastefully frisky or officiously attentive with you, make them a sandwich of the same ingredients, uttering a few words to the effect of "Back!" as you make it. If they eat the leaves, they will begin to take on the idea that their flirtations are unwelcome.

THINKING UP A BARRIER

The most important place to begin your siege warfare—and keep another out of your garden—is in your head. As with all magic, a practical assessment of the situation should be followed by a symbolic refusal of continuance magically (and, as relevant, a physical barrier being placed between you and the other party). Your mind can do much of this work by carefully aimed thought. Here your visualization skills are in demand. You must harness what you learned in chapters 1 and 2 and concentrate your thoughts on gently but firmly refusing the advances that you don't want. Employ the colors and scents of refusal, and send a powerful, polite request to the other party to cease their actions.

DISCOURAGING YOUR OWN FEELINGS. From time to time, temptations arise to provoke the most constant of lovers. It may be that you are part of a normally happy pair, but that someone else has simply stolen your attention momentarily. Or possibly your own partner is too busy to pay you proper due. Or, you are tired, lonely, or in need of an ego boost.

In such situations, sit down and discuss with yourself (a) what is the cause of your new interest in someone else and (b) whether or not this will ultimately cost you all that you love. Sometimes, just pausing and assessing what you will lose, or what pain you may be entering into, is enough to dissuade you (at least mentally) from active pursuit of the tempting new personality.

This may be one of the most important things you will ever do to save yourself immense pain, hurt, and mischief. Scent your room with mint and one other fragrance chosen from those described on page 77, light one pink and one white candle, and tie several white ribbons around the room. Find a piece of hawthorn, or rose thorn if you have no access to a thorn tree, and place it between the two candles.

Now imagine the other person's face and pretend you can see it through the ring of your thorn knot. Send it love, but send it also a warning not to get any closer. Give yourself the same mental warning. Breathe in the scent of restraint, tie a white ribbon around your wrist or finger, and padlock your consciousness to the other person by literally envisioning a padlock on your heart.

Then dispel your own amorous feelings by quietly drawing the other person to mind, fixing on one (perhaps the only) part of their physical appearance or personality that you don't like, and exaggerating its importance in your mind. If you don't much like their nose, for example, magnify it into a caricature of itself—so that it makes you laugh. Or, if you don't like the way they dress, exaggerate this style.

Finally, send the person a feeling of good friendship, so that you avoid the idea that they are "forbidden fruit." Make sure that you congratulate yourself on your very strong will— and do not be afraid to recognize that it is an act of will to terminate your feelings.

If you can spend sufficient time on this now, and truly talk yourself out of any attraction, you may save a great deal of worry and ensure instead a future of genuine, warm friendship.

OTHER TIPS

- If you are concerned that someone in your office is getting ideas about you, spritz a little camphor oil blended with one or two of the other oils described on page 77 and spray this around your desk. Tie a white ribbon around your chair to keep yourself "free" from others. Place a pink candle scented with your chosen anti-attractant near your front door and then light it, asking (anyone in particular, or everyone in general) respecfully to keep their distance from you.

- Spray your car with the above mixture to keep thieves away. Do the same to your flowerpots and garden beds to communicate your lack of hospitality to cats and dogs.

- Wearing pink and/or white clothes is a good shield against attention; if you have an appointment with someone you don't wish to encourage, wear these colors and place a thorn knot in your pocket. Donning some scent made up from three of those described on page 77 will seal the fatal unattraction!

- If you feel that you are "under siege" from someone who is taking liberties with you in their thoughts, place a beautiful sprig of blossoming hawthorn, or a knot woven from the tree, above your front door, tied into a rose-pink or pinky-white silk kerchief. This is also a good safeguard against theft. If you tie a willow twig in with it, intruders will come to no good end if they cross your threshold!

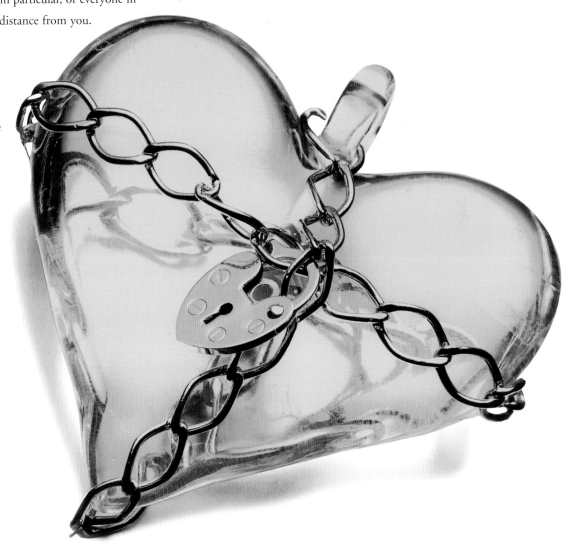

MASTER SPELL: TO DISENCHANT A PAST LOVER OR UNWANTED ADMIRER.
If you want to ease away someone who has impossible hopes for either a renewed relationship with you or a cherished but completely unreturned interest in your affection, perform this spell with feeling, but firm denial.

YOU WILL NEED

3 rose-pink and 3 white candles; a few drops of pine and camphor oils (substitute another second choice if you cannot find camphor); a piece of hawthorn cut from a living tree; a very small blank notebook, with your "harasser's" name written on the first page; a photograph of the person, if you have one, or an item belonging to them if not; a sprig of peppermint (fresh grown, or bought packaged from the supermarket); a small birdcage, or other pet cage (even a nesting box would do, as long as it has a door you can leave open); 1 yard each of pink and white ribbon.

MOON PHASE: *Work on a full moon, and finish the spell within 24 hours so that the moon is waning by the end of the period.*

Form a large triangle shape with the candles, to symbolize that there are effectively three people in this spell: you, the unwanted lover, and another person to whom you would like your admirer to transfer their affection. Anoint the candles with a drop of each oil a few minutes before you light them, and say the name of your "harasser" as you do this. Take the thorn, tied in a large ring-shaped knot, and pass it over each candle in turn, saying firmly, *"[name], take your affections and burn for another; Though I will be friends I cannot be your lover. I wish you well with somebody new, But there can be nothing between me and you."* IMAGINE KISSING THE PERSON VERY CHASTELY, AND SEE YOURSELF WALKING AWAY.

While the candles burn, write the person's name in the notebook, sprinkle oils onto the page, and tape in the photograph or item belonging to them. Draw a wing upon the page, to symbolize flight from each other, and imagine the person running swiftly away from you to another life. Pass the peppermint and the thorn knot through the light of the candles, repeat the words, then place the peppermint in the notebook near the name and photo. Look at the picture and slip the "ring" of thorn onto your marriage finger; explain in your own words that this union, so desired by the other, is not wished for by you. Slip off the thorn ring and place it on the page, open.

Finally, put the notebook into the little cage, and leave the door open. Visualize one last, powerful image of the person who likes you departing from the cage they have made for themselves in wanting your love, and ask that they fly out. Sprinkle the cage with a little of the oil.

The next day, take the notebook and tie it with the ribbons, enclosing all that has gone inside (photo, name, oils, peppermint sprig—but not the hawthorn). Place the "ring" on your finger one last time, and take the book to moving water. Imagine you are freeing a caged bird as you drop the book in the water and watch it rush away. Take the "ring" off your finger and say the words opposite one last time. See the bond depart; see the other party freed, and you as well. WISH THEM WELL ELSEWHERE.

VARIATIONS ON THE MASTER SPELL

TO DISENCHANT A COMPETITOR FROM BORROWING YOUR LOVER.

YOU WILL NEED

Candles, a piece of hawthorn and a notebook, as before; the name of your competitor written on a small piece of paper; a few drops of grapefruit oil, as before; a piece of string or fine twisted cord.

In the morning or evening on a waning moon, place your rival's name under the candles, sprinkle grapefruit oil on the paper, and encircle the candles with the hawthorn. See the face of your opposition in the flames and ask that they move on; imagine your beloved waving them goodbye. Be gentle and kind, but firm; wish them luck with another (new) lover. Imagine the barrier forming between your love and the intruder, and see this barrier as a hedge of hawthorn. Now put a few drops of oil and a piece of the hawthorn on the first page of the notebook, and write the name of your rival nearby. Close the book, and tie it with the string or twisted cord. Wish your rival happiness—elsewhere. Extinguish the candles, and wave the book through the smoke. Toss it in a moving stream of water .... *Goodbye!*

☽

TO DISENCHANT HARASSMENT AT THE OFFICE, here is a full variant, almost a new second spell, for what is after all a delicate and not uncommon problem.

YOU WILL NEED
Leave out the birdcage; substitute for the oils a few drops of grapefruit oil; you will need only one of the ribbons, so choose the color you prefer; add a paper clip from the office and the name of the firm, or work address, written on a small piece of paper.

The night before you go to work, light the six candles and say the name of the person who is harassing you. Place the bramble, tied loosely into a knot (handle carefully) around the candles, and ask that the person (say their name) keep their respectful distance from your private life and feelings, while working with cordiality. Imagine a healthy barrier coming between you, with an atmosphere of unemotive respect growing stronger. Extinguish the candles. The following morning, dab some grapefruit oil on the ribbon, then take the hawthorn knot and sprig of peppermint and put them on your office desk, or wherever they will be seen by your clingy hopeful.

Breathe in the light from the previous night and adopt an air of calm control. Now use the paper clip to place the person's name, the sprig of peppermint, and the firm's name inside the opening page of the little book. Wish them a happy voyage with a new person—a new chapter opening for them, but not with *you*. Later that night, light the candles once more and again put the hawthorn around them. Imagine that you have an impenetrable barrier around you, and your persistent harasser cannot harm you. Tie up the notebook with the ribbon, blow out the candles, and sleep soundly. Your problems are already diminished. If necessary, repeat seven days later.

TO KEEP INTRUSIVE ANIMALS AWAY FROM YOUR CHILDREN AND PLANTS.

YOU WILL NEED
A decoction made with 6 drops of grapefruit and 4 drops of peppermint essential oil, blended with almond oil; a pink ribbon.

Spray the oil directly onto the garden patch, or grass, or your child's clothing, to dissuade animals from hanging around. Tie the pink ribbon, dowsed in the oil mixture, onto some of the flowers, or the garden gate, or your child's wrist. This will help to prevent animals from getting too close.

NOTE: If you feel seriously threatened by someone's attentions—perhaps these are bordering on stalking—protect your person and environment daily by cleansing with white light, as described in chapter 1. Do this in tandem with the disenchantment spells, but, obviously, also seek professional advice.

THIS

CHAPTER CENTERS ON THE MOST IMPORTANT

OF ALL THE MOONS—OAK, THE MOON OF STRENGTH AND

SECURITY. THIS IS THE MOMENT IN THE YEAR WHEN THE SUN HAS

REACHED ITS ZENITH; WE ARE IN THE DOMAIN OF THE LONGEST DAY. WE WILL

EXAMINE MAGIC FOR PROTECTION AND SECURITY, ESPECIALLY FINANCIAL SECURITY,

AND WORK A MASTER SPELL FOR FERTILITY. WE ADOPT TALISMANS FOR EVERYDAY POWER AND

PERSONAL STRENGTH, MANY OF WHICH TAKE THEIR INSPIRATION FROM THE MIGHTY OAK

TREE. ANCIENT RITUALS CONNECTED WITH MIDSUMMER, THE SOLSTICE (ON JUNE 21, WITHIN

7:SECURITY

THE PERIOD—EARLY JUNE TO EARLY JULY—

RULED BY THIS MOON), AND THE CERTAINTY

OF A GOOD CROP CAME UNDER THE AEGIS OF THIS MOON. THE EARTH WAS PREGNANT, BUT THE

SAFE DELIVERY OF A HEALTHY AND BOUNTIFUL HARVEST HAD TO BE WORKED FOR. THUS IN LIFE,

WE MUST NOT REST ON OUR LAURELS, BUT PERPETUALLY PUT IN THE EFFORT TO ASSURE

CONTINUING STRENGTH AND SURETY. THIS IS THE TIME OF YEAR DEDICATED TO

CULTIVATING AND APPLYING OUR KNOWLEDGE FOR UTMOST SECURITY. THE MONTH

OF JUNE WAS NAMED "OAK" ("DUIR") IN THE CELTIC CALENDAR, AND JUNO

WAS THE CONSORT OF JUPITER, WHO WAS ASSOCIATED WITH THE

OAK—THE KING OF TREES. THUS HER EMBLEM IS THE JUNE—

MIDSUMMER—MOON, WHILE HIS IS THE OAK

SUN.

OAK MOON—MOON OF STRENGTH AND SECURITY. Colors: BRICK, EARTH, WHITE. Scents: GERANIUM, BAY, FRANKINCENSE, SANDALWOOD. Number: 7. The oak is tried and true; its wood is dense and close-grown, and it endures for several hundred years growing in the forest; similarly, its wood is the strongest and most enduring for building. Thus the tree is a symbol of strength, wisdom, endurance, and security. Oak wood is the most powerful fuel of fire and is seen in conjunction with the most powerful sun—THE "SECURE" SUN!

"She kneels beneath the huge oak tree
And in silence prayeth she."
"CHRISTABEL"
SAMUEL TAYLOR COLERIDGE

The subject of personal security embraces many things: it could include self-confidence, financial stability, happiness in love, a safe place in which to live; but in the specific realm of the witches' working calendar, this security is most strongly related to the protection of home and family and financial security. Tied in with this is the concept at the heart of the number "7" (for this is the seventh moon), which is concerned with the intellect and analysis—qualities that are directly involved with the maintenance of financial security.

For centuries in Pagan magic and worship, oak bark, acorns, and leaves have been used medicinally, as well as in fertility rites, divination magic, and prosperity and protection magic.

The oak could almost be equated with anything positive: for this reason, the acorn is often used as a central motif in all types of spell, and for the magical path that represents magic in our everyday lives. Oak was the most sacred tree of all to the Druids, and in many English churches the vaulting is made from curved oak timbers; indeed, the columns of the nave seem almost to resemble overhanging branches in a great forest. This perhaps recalls the time when the forest was actually the religious grove of Druid worship: nature herself was the venerated force.

This, then, is the time to employ nature to the full and venerate our own life force—our strength, security, and positivity. By doing this effectively, we can turn our lives along a route of good fortune and sunshine. If thought is the most powerful element we have with which to direct our future, we must think up powerfully positive thoughts to determine the extent of our happiness, inner calm, and power to attain.

As with all magic, the effectiveness of your magic-making will depend on your capacity to think powerful thoughts and to visualize well. By now you will have become more used to doing this as part of spell-making; you should find the exercise of sending protective light in conjunction with spells for security very easy to achieve. *If we think positively, we can design for ourselves the lives we want ….*

BEGINNING WITH THOUGHT

To be adept, our thoughts must be well directed, focused, and unflinching. Begin by releasing any negativity from the past. Do not castigate yourself for previous failures or weaknesses, but go past them. Remind yourself that burning a cake once does not mean you will always do so: you have learned more about what will make the cake burn, so you can improve the next try.

So IN MAGIC: let go completely of past misfortunes, cease to think of yourself in any negative way at all, and set your course for a more fulfilled and prosperous future. Certain scents will help you do this; so will color. Strangely enough, beating past failures is often simply a case of assessing an impasse quickly and letting go of the dead wood, rather than hanging on to "no-win" situations. It may also be largely a matter of making the decision to go out and meet life, rather than expecting everything to come to you on a platter. If you take a shining, positive face out into the world, you will soon discover that you meet with a more positive response from all around you.

Move toward greater strength in your life, armed with talismans for positivity, by being decisive in small projects and taking gentle, unhurried steps toward attaining each one. You will make no progress if you set yourself no goals. The adage that you get more out of life if you put more in is, simply, all too true!

SCENTS FOR OPTIMISM

Many scents are associated with making us feel more positive; the woody aromas, such as pine, cedar, rosewood, and cypress, are all scents that help us to feel clear-headed, secure, and well grounded. But if you want to surround yourself with scents that have a traditional role in positive thought, those valued in the East—frankincense and sandalwood—can make you feel quite inspirational. It is worth using a diffuser, or scented candles, in conjunction with sending your light and thinking positively.

So, a simple routine for preparing the ground for a successful, secure situation would be as follows. Consider the end product you would like to reach: if you are timid about a meeting, an interview, a date, an exam, a social occasion, a speech you have to give, or whatever, think clearly about arriving—or receiving a guest—with a sense of total self-confidence, poise and inner security. Now diffuse one of the above oils into the atmosphere from a burner, or bathe in a combination of several, and inhale deeply, calmly, confidently, and rhythmically while focusing on the desired outcome. By doing this, you are preparing the way—rehearsing, if you like—for the real thing.

Geranium and bay are also wonderful scents for strength, optimism, and security. If you are performing in a play, taking a driving test—anything, in fact, where you need to feel sure of yourself—dilute these (a few drops of each in a base oil, such as sweet almond) and wear them on your wrist or as a perfume. *You will be shining, confident, and focused from beginning to end!*

THE COLORS OF POSITIVITY AND STRENGTH

Well might you expect to see the colors of positivity and security coming from the brilliant primaries, or bold, bright colors. In fact, interestingly, the colors associated with strength are the colors of the earth—the browns, especially brick. Is it because they connote solidity, dependability, rather than passing dazzle? I don't know the answer, but earth colors definitely make us feel secure. Wearing browns can make us feel more grounded and reliable. Use a shade of brown that speaks to you; "brick" could go all the way to a Chinese brick red!

When you are sallying forth into the world and want to feel secure and optimistic, apart from wearing browns you could tie ribbons in the brownish hues all about you: on your wrist, in your car, on your briefcase or purse. Don't worry if it seems eccentric: this translates to others as difference and creativity!

MIDSUMMER FEAST

The reasoning behind the celebration of midsummer is the vigilance of prayer that the earth—now pregnant—carries well and bears a fruitful crop. You can no doubt see the correlation between this idea and all the magical concepts of the chapter for security, positivity, and success. This, then, is the moment to light the fires of protection and see a sound conclusion to a job well done in the months ahead.

Simple celebrations abound. You might honor the oak— and in conjunction, security and dependability—by tying a ribbon (not yellow) around an old oak tree. Kiss the tree as you do so, and thank the earth for your home. Promise to be more aware of others who need little blessings in any shape or form.

If you are lucky enough to find an oak with holy MISTLETOE growing on its boughs, this is the moment to cut some and honor the spirit of the gods. Mistletoe was the most prized herb of the Druids, and it is inseparable from the oak. It is of course a symbol of fertility—the white berries might help you to imagine why this is so. If you and a friend can find some, take a clean knife (never used before) on midsummer day and cut off a bough of mistletoe with a prayer of thanks and a wish to the universe for prosperity. Taking the plant into your home will bring the good luck and strength in with you!

Set trestle tables out of doors at midsummer and honor the beautiful, resilient, wise earth. See yourself within its vibration: as a breeze blows, think how it affects you. Invite friends to the feast, asking each to bring a plate of outdoor food. Always include some herb-based treat: I like to serve sorrel tartlets, or lavender-flavored meats. Have a choice of desserts that celebrate the fruit harvests of summer: berries of all types. Wines, equally, might be rather unusual, based on flowers or berries instead of the grape. And do have some music, of any kind: this honors vibratory positivity in a unique way.

- Pin a sprig of mistletoe, holly (for the holly, or waning, year will now take over from the oak as we move toward the shortest day), hazel, or oak to your jacket or dress, and make one positive wish.

- Sit and read a friend's *I Ching*, or the *Oraqle*, or tarot. Divination shared is especially favored, and will be full of insight, at this moment of optimum lucidity in the year.

- Plant one new tree in the garden, or buy one decent new potted plant (on a reasonably large scale) for your home, and consecrate it to the gods. Nurture it, and see it as a communication line to them.

- Tie brick-red and white ribbons everywhere: on gateposts, park benches, doors, cars, chairs—anywhere. Spread love as you tie.

- Buy a pet, or bless an existing one, at this time. Blessing can be done by sprinkling rainwater gently on the animal's head. Stroke the animal and send it love and strength.

- Place something new (a crystal, perhaps, or a candlestick, or a vase) in your home, and see it as an emblem of strength.

- Phone past friends, and invite them over.

All these things are acts of recognition to the earth for what it gives, and an attempt to put something back. Choose your own ideas and ways of expressing yourself—but do honor the day, and be aware from here on of your need for positivity and truth.

SECURITY MAGIC IN EVERYDAY LIFE. You can incorporate the symbology of the oak moon into your daily life to encourage a positive outcome on a regular basis. NEVER LEAVE HOME WITHOUT AN ACORN!

This powerful talisman is sure to attract growing strength in your life. If you can't get hold of a real one, ask a jeweler to make you one in silver or gold. Put it in your pocket, tie it to your key ring, attach it to your purse or billfold, or place it in a prominent place at the office or in your home. Charge it first with real strength from a full summery moon—oak if possible—and imagine beautiful light filling the little acorn, infusing it with power and strength. Think of this little "battery," full of energy, now being in your control.

CHOOSE ANY WAY OF PLACING THIS POWERFUL TALISMAN IN YOUR LIFE THAT FITS IN WITH YOUR LIFESTYLE.

- Soak in a bath of oak leaves, and draw in (almost hypnotically) a feeling of control and inner power. If you can get some oak bark, you will find bathing in it very therapeutic: *the bark has a long history of use as a medicine with antiseptic and astringent properties.*

- It may be possible to find acorn-shaped finials for drapery or shade pulls, because the oak tree has long been associated with protection of the house, particularly from thunder and lightning, because it was dedicated to the Scandinavian god Thor.

- Design your own jewelry around acorns, oak leaves, or oak wood, and pin it as a brooch for an added boost.

- Decorate your house with oak motifs, for continuing strength and positivity. Gather oak leaves at an appropriate time, spray them gold if you wish, and put them on plates; make place mats with them, or press them in a picture frame.

- Find an old piece of oak wood and incorporate that into your interior theme. This would also be wonderful with acorns added to it, sprayed gold or silver, and ribbons tied around, perhaps with candles. It could then function as a permanent altar dedicated to wisdom, strength, security, positivity, and intellect.

GROW AN OAK TREE!

This might sound a bit ambitious, but you can do it in a number of ways. You might begin with a small pot, and put it on a balcony or terrace, beside a front door, or on a windowsill. You might ask your local government if they would let you plant one in a park; then, you could visit it regularly and regard it as yours. You might ask a friend who has a garden to lend you space to "sponsor" an oak tree; or, you might just "adopt" one growing nearby in a park where you can go and sit under it, think around it, "breathe" it in. If all this really is impossible (if you haven't even got access to a park, for example), then paint an oak tree on a wall in your apartment, or even on a canvas, positioning it somewhere central in your home. TAKE ON THE STRENGTH OF AN OAK TREE, IN ANY WAY YOU CAN.

MAKING A PROTECTIVE RING AROUND YOUR HOUSE. One way of adding security to your life is to perform an overall protection spell to place in your home. This will have the effect of denying easy access to bad spirits and keeping you, as the dweller therein, optimistic. As with the birch rituals in chapter 1, the circle is the most appropriate means of achieving this.

- If you are building a house from the ground up, put an acorn or oak leaf under the foundation stone, and say a prayer to the earth to protect you and the dwelling. Then walk once around the stone clockwise, and "charm" the earth under your feet with words of appreciation. Make them personal.

- When you move into a new house, and while it is still empty prior to your moving your furniture and possessions into the space, walk around each room in turn in a large clockwise circle, and sprinkle one of the oils listed on page 89 to secure the house for positivity. If you need to purify as well (for instance, if there has been an unhappy previous owner), sprinkle some rose oil in the circle and place one red candle in the window on the first night.

- If your apartment is small, or you are already living there and just want to begin securing it now, make a circle of white lights with little votive candles in your main living area, and sit in the middle holding some oak, an acorn, a leaf—or even just a brown ribbon if you can't get anything oaky! Sprinkle the oil of one of your chosen scents (see page 89) in front of you, and breathe in a whole new state of being. Determine in your mind that life will begin to go smoothly, and that you will complete your projects, tasks, and goals with grace and strength. Keep the candles burning for about ten minutes while you visualize; then take each one to a different room and place a small flower beside it. Light each candle from time to time when you feel the need to rev up your positivity battery a little.

- If you are being really witchy, fill a bottle with some fresh earth (from a garden center, perhaps), place a lock of your hair in it, cork it, and wrap with a brick or brown and white ribbon. Walk once around the bottle in a circle, then encircle your own body with the bottle held at arm's length and place it in a corner, either close to your hearth (if you have a fireplace) or perhaps near a potted plant. This recalls the ancient belief that a bad spirit had to count every grain of earth before taking up residence in a house. It would take a very long time to count the whole bottle, and the spirit might lose count several times and have to start again, so it would eventually give up!

- My own favorite method of drawing security and positivity into a dwelling (and a life) is to knot an old key—clock keys are wonderfully theatrical—with a piece of brown and white ribbon, looping in an acorn as well (pierce the acorn with a needle and thread string or thread through it). THIS LOOKS QUITE BEAUTIFUL, AND BOTH THE KEY AND THE ACORN ARE SYMBOLIC OF STRENGTH.

MASTER SPELL 1: TO DRAW FINANCIAL AND PERSONAL STRENGTH AND POSITIVITY. This spell works very well to draw security, strength, and optimism into any area of your life. It might be required for financial certainty or as a general wish, or for a new relationship just getting off the ground which you want to progress with confidence and optimism.

YOU WILL NEED
A brick-red ribbon or cord; frankincense, sandalwood, or bay oil (or a blend of all three); a handful of oak leaves; your choice of candles; a crystal; a wooden or silver chalice filled with rainwater; 7 long stems of different-colored flowers (whatever is in season).

MOON PHASE: *Waxing.*

Prepare by taking an oak bath. Tie the brick-red ribbon or cord around the faucets to "color" and power the water, and run the bath, adding 6–8 drops each of two or three of the oils at the end, and finally floating the oak leaves around the bath. Bathe by candlelight—the size, number, and color of the candles can be absolutely your own choice.

As you soak up the lovely leaves, envision exactly what it is that you hope for. Slide down into the water and close your eyes; see if you can "feel" a kind of force field around you, and visualize yourself victorious in your hopes within the power and light of this tremendous energy. Breathe in the oils, and say, *"Charge my spirit, cleanse my soul; Fill my life with happiness whole."* Take in the ideas and fill your senses from the eyes, the nose, the skin, the ears: THIS IS THE SWEET SMELL OF SUCCESS!

After your bath, sit in the candlelight and place the crystal into the rainwater-filled chalice, once again seeing security and continuance of all you hold dear—even an improvement in your affairs—but hold on tight to the one special thing you wish for.

If this concerns money and business, see steady success, rather than greedy piles of profit! Sure steps are what you are asking for. If your spell primarily concerns a relationship growing more secure, don't immediately expect commitments, but see a steady growth of communication, trust, interest, depth of feeling, and confidence. If you like, imagine you see all this in the ether of the light or in the crystal and chalice.

Finally, place the chalice (with the crystal inside) next to the flowers, and imagine all seven—the rainbow of colors—filling the cup with every shade of knowledge, growth, and strength. Untie the ribbon from the bath faucets, and place it around the chalice. Make a small, personally worded prayer for steady judgment and growing positivity.

Leave the items in place for 24 hours, and repeat the spell once more when the moon is again waxing—perhaps a month (or two) later. The power supply of positivity around you is now at its fullest!

MASTER SPELL 11: **TO AID FERTILITY.** This spell is also for use under the power of the oak moon. In high summer the earth is at its most pregnant, and petitions for personal fertility can be very effective at this time. If it seems just too wishful to imagine that a fertility spell will make you pregnant—especially if you've been trying for a while—just remember that many people agree that the mind, as well as the body, plays a part in conception, and that some women do get pregnant when the moment feels absolutely right. This spell is to help your body feel just that—and though it won't work miracles, it may push your mindset into a higher gear.

YOU WILL NEED
Fertility herbs: cuttings of willow and oak, or acorns, seeds of parsley, coriander, and Florence fennel; 1 white, 3 pink, and 3 blue candles.

MOON PHASE: *New.*

At sunset on a new moon during the summer period (but not necessarily at midsummer itself), plant any three of the above herbs in three patches to represent god, goddess, and earth, and father, mother, and child. Water in the seeds, asking for the great fecund earth to bring life to you and your partner, and as you sow the parsley—which germinates very slowly and is a symbol of patience regarding conception—imagine your own (or your partner's) body swelling with life and filled with green growth.

Mark each seed patch with a tiny candle (one each in blue, white, and pink), and trace a triangle in the earth. Four candles remain—two blue and two pink. Light these alternately over the four weeks following your seed planting, during which time you should get busy with your sexual contribution to fertility! AS THE SEEDS SPROUT, YOUR BODY SHOULD COME INTO ITS OWN CLOCK, AND IMAGINING SUCCESS MAY MAKE THE BIGGEST DIFFERENCE TO YOUR CHANCES OF CONCEIVING.

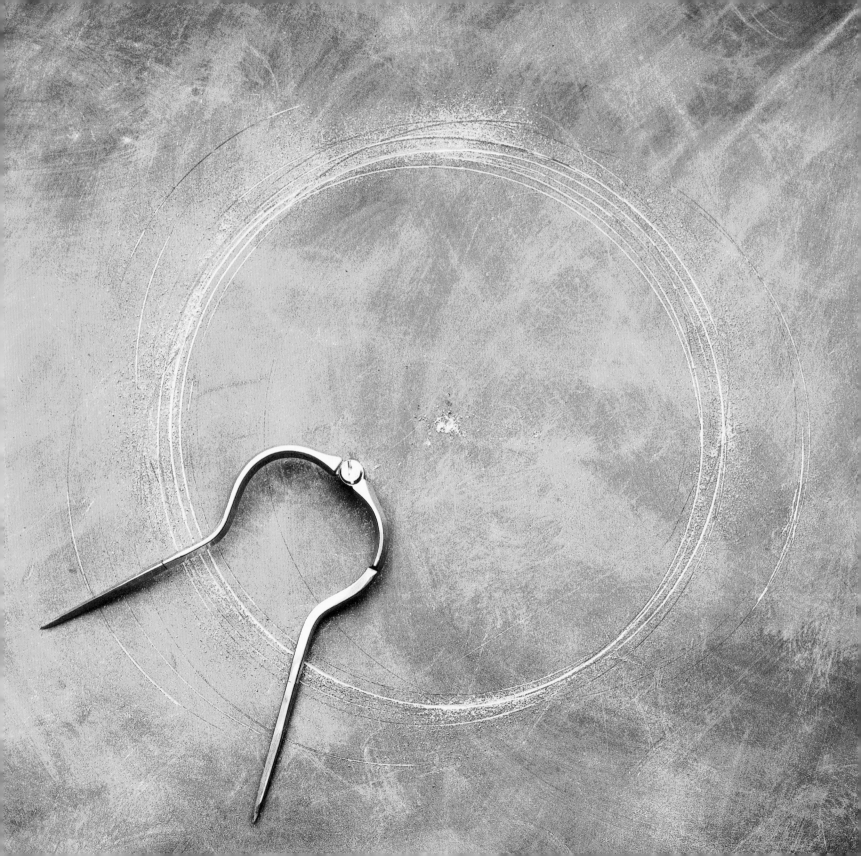

THERE

ARE TIMES WHEN ONE LONGS TO BE ABLE TO

TURN THE CLOCK BACK. THE BEAUTIFUL, SERRATED HOLLY

LEAF IS VERY IMPORTANT IN THIS CHAPTER, WHICH IS ABOUT REVERSING

DIFFICULT SITUATIONS. UNHAPPY WORDS AND TENSE RELATIONSHIPS CAN BE

"UNWISHED" OR "UN-SAID" BY CHANGING THEIR "POLARITY"; RESCUES CAN OCCUR

(METAPHORICALLY) EVEN BEFORE A SITUATION HAS REACHED THE POINT OF HARMFUL

IMPACT. HERE WE LEARN THE MAGIC REQUIRED TO REVERSE A PROBLEMATIC SITUATION THAT

IS STILL VIABLE. IF THERE IS A BUSINESS THREAT, OR A HEALTH PROBLEM ARISING, OR

8: ENCIRCLEMENT — EVEN A DIFFICULTY STARTING TO AFFECT

A LOVE RELATIONSHIP, THE HOLLY MOON IS THE ONE THAT CAN GOVERN TURNING THINGS AROUND

180 DEGREES. THIS EVEN STRETCHES TO INCLUDE A SPELL AGAINST GOSSIPING! THIS MOON

INCLUDES THE SABBAT OF LUGHNASADH (OR LAMMAS) ON AUGUST 1–2, WHICH WAS A GRAIN

FESTIVAL; AND MAKING FLOWER DOLLS AND CORN DOLLS IS PART OF THE MAGIC ELEMENT OF

HONORING THIS TIME. THE HOLLY MOON—THE MOON OF POLARITY ("IF I COULD

TURN BACK TIME...")—COVERS THE PERIOD EARLY JULY TO EARLY AUGUST.

IT IS THE REVERSAL OF SUMMER, WHEN THE DAYS LEAD INEXORABLY

TOWARD WINTER AND THE HIGH MOMENT OF THE HOLLY

KING—WHO IS ONE MODEL FOR SANTA

CLAUSE.

Holly Moon—Moon of Encirclement and Polarity. Color: Bronze, Sunshine Yellow. Scent: Coriander, Tuberose, Benzoin. Number: 8. There comes a moment when, no matter how much positive magic you have worked toward any one situation, life and events seem destined to take their own course and career down a path that is out of your control.

"O! Call back yesterday, bid time return."
Richard II, Act 3 Scene ii,
William Shakespeare

Perhaps in a relationship, despite careful tending and real effort, an inevitable misunderstanding or flash of careless anger threatens to dismantle everything you have worked for. Perhaps a business, which you have nurtured, now shows signs of fatigue; or another goal in business or your career which you have been steadily moving toward suddenly appears to be out of reach, or beyond your hopes. This is the moment to work "polarity magic."

Polarity can also be seen as a rebalancing: a situation has gone too far in one direction and must be brought back the other way. As with all magic, some of this can be done with the deft use of physical ingredients (oils, herbs, and colors), while much of it is achieved through the powerful concentration of the mind, which exerts a dedicated magnetic pull to draw a situation gently back from its current (errant!) position. You must believe with all your might that you can effect this response.

Celebrating Lammas

The Pagan festival of Lammas is a celebration of the first fruits of the harvest—an early crop. The word itself derives from "Hlafmas," an Anglo-Saxon word which translates as the "loaf mass." This refers to the importance of the grain, and is a celebration of the first picking of wheat. In the Irish tradition, the god Lugh is associated with this festival, and the day called Lughnasadh. It is a Celtic moon festival, and can be recognized even in the Roman moon goddess, Luna.

The key aspects of the celebration are concerned with corn dolls, grain ales, the waning moon as well as the idea of a buried treasure in the earth! As the grain is harvested, so the earth's progeny dies; implicit in this death, however, is the polar concept that in spring all will be reborn.

To make good earth magic, and to bless your own workings over the course of the coming winter days, ensuring re-emergence into sunshine and fecundity again, work with friends to bake special loaves of unusual breads which will recognize the importance of this simple grain. If you have a taste for whisky, which was traditional and sacred to this festival, try sampling something special and toasting the friends around you. Make wishes as you sip! Otherwise, if beers are more pleasing to your palate, make an informal feast out of corn chips and a few glasses of your favorite brew.

Weave a corn doll from a bronze-yellow sheaf of wheat, and make strong wishes as you go. It is also traditional to braid a semicircular tiara and dedicate it to the Earth Mother. If you have the patience to make corn muffins, or corn bread, throw the leftover crumbs to the birds and make a blessing, which in turn ensures your own good fortune.

Since Lammas is still a period of peak growth in the garden, and flowers are as beautiful as ever at this moment, flower dolls can be made as decoration for the tables. Using the colors bronze and sunshine yellow, make a doll from any scented herbage, incorporating yellow pansies and sunflowers, or small yellow daisies. Use wire to get a good shape, and secure the joins with ribbon. Weave a dream as you work, and sing. This lucky talisman may be the key to your dream coming true: so preserve it in a dried form after the month has long passed.

HARVEST CORN CAKE

YOU WILL NEED

1 cup of all-purpose flour; 1/4 cup of sugar; 1 teaspoon of baking soda; 1 teaspoon of baking powder; a pinch of salt; 1 cup of yellow cornmeal; 1 large beaten egg; 1 cup of fromage blanc; 2 tablespoons of butter; melted; 1 tablespoon of molasses.

Sift together the flour, sugar, baking soda, baking powder, and salt in a medium-sized mixing bowl. Add the cornmeal and mix well. Make a well in the center, and, using a knife, mix in the egg, the fromage blanc and butter to a smooth consistency. Lastly, mix in the molasses. Beat all the ingredients until smooth, but do not over-process. Place the mixture in a well-greased loaf or square pan, and bake at 400°F for about 20–25 minutes. Serve warm with butter.

COUNTERACTIVE MAGIC. It may be that your life has now reached a moment when you want to turn everything around and begin to travel in the opposite direction. This kind of magic should creep into everyday life; it is prescribed when, for example, every relationship you have had seems to have ended in disappointment or failure.

If, perpetually, you begin a love affair with someone and everything is going well, only to suddenly and inexplicably enter a bad patch and end, you need to work polarity magic. Maybe you always reach a point where you believe things must go wrong—because they always have in the past! It is time to turn the clock around and go the other way.

This can be just as true in your business, career, or working life. Perhaps you have always reached a particular point and then failed to make the very highest grade because you said something tactless, or maybe you simply don't feel secure enough to push yourself forward any further. You must see yourself as a success, and dispel the feeling of being doomed to repeated failure. Indeed, if you have any repetition of events that you would like to change—lapses into arguments with friends and in-laws, perhaps, or bad luck, or even ongoing ailments with the same theme (like repeated colds)—you need to work on the magnetic opposite.

COUNTERACTIVE MAGIC IN EVERYDAY LIFE

If you need to arrest a downward slide in any area of your life, you must work very hard to turn things around mentally. This amounts to a kind of psychological reconditioning: but this is partly what magic is about.

Begin by cleansing your environment. Spin a nest of bright yellow or bronze-sunshine colored light around the room(s) in your mind's eye, first in a clockwise direction, then counterclockwise, to show an "unwinding" of what has gone before. Place a small magnet in the room.

Scent the room(s) with coriander and benzoin oils, and add a drop or two of tuberose if you have it. These oils are associated with transformation, balance, and self-forgiveness—the last of which is sometimes the easiest to overlook when you need to overcome a negative spiral. If matters continually seem to degenerate, or you feel you have messed up an otherwise good situation, it is essential to forgive yourself and move on.

COMPASS

A compass (with cardinal points) is a symbol associated with the desire to change direction in a situation. If this emblem appeals to you, try writing a letter of apology to someone you have fallen out with and enclose a compass in the envelope to signify a new wind blowing through your minds, ushering you both to calmer climes. Or, perhaps you wish to turn around a business that is floundering, or an academic course which is not going the way you would like it to. Firstly, you must cleanly envision a new, more positive direction emerging in your business or study life; then, taking some appropriate paperwork, put a beautiful compass into a folder with the papers and tie them up with a yellow ribbon. As you do this, visualize a change: see negativity replaced with positive results.

THE ANGEL OF MERCY

A very effective way of visualizing the "undoing" of a bad situation is to see, in your mind's eye, an angel of mercy, or a bright, positive fairy figure, stepping in and preventing the last steps that led to the fatally angry words, or the breakup, or the aborted opportunity.

If, for instance, you want to "take back" something you wish you had never said or done, follow the scenting and cleansing regime on page 102, and then vividly imagine their presence just prior to the problematic moment. Now see the angel figure shrouding you and the other person (or people) concerned with beautiful light and arresting the damaging words or actions before they occur. Imagine, vividly, a different outcome: see a happier resolution, and pass the wounded party a small magnet with a sunshine-yellow bow tied around it, either in your mind's eye, or—all the better—in reality when you can. This could take the form of a letter or card sent through the mail with a magnet, thus tied, enclosed. Whatever words you write, make them brief, and let the magnet with the silent, powerful message do the work. Imagine the angel in your mind's eye preparing the ground for the letter or card to arrive: instead of a mailman, see an angel delivering your note; and visualize an angel embracing, mollifying, and caressing the party who will be the recipient of your token of reversal. Imagine saying, *"These words, that action (etc.) were never said: I had the sense to stop short of saying (or, if the other said the harsh words, hearing) them."*

MAGNETS

If you are about to go for a job interview after a run of rejections; take an exam after a long period of undesirable results; take a driving test for the umpteenth time; go on a date with a new love interest after a long period of non-starters; or anything where you wish to turn around an ongoing series of disappointments—take with you in your pocket or purse a magnet, tied with yellow ribbon, into which you have poured powerful, positive mental energy along with a wish for a reversal of fortune.

If your car has been costing you too much money, or has often been banged into or even stolen, put a magnet—exactly as above—in the glove compartment.

If you wish to reverse bad luck in a relationship, or even a breakup, place a tiny magnet in an ice-cube tray along with the name of the person you want to heal the bond with, and put it in the freezer with these words: *"A change of luck, A change of direction, May our bond undergo more positive protection."*

HOLLY

A sprig of holly, or a holly leaf, makes a talisman with a similar effect to that of a magnet; however, it is a better choice if the reversal you want to achieve concerns sharp words that have passed between you and a lover, friend, employer, family member, or whomever. Place a photograph of yourself and the wounded (or offended) party on a small table, or in a little box or basket, surrounded by eight holly leaves. Meanwhile, burn a bronze or yellow candle nearby, and gently say that you are sorry for your own part in the misunderstanding or argument that has befallen you both. Ask for tolerance and a chance to set things right.

If the situation is really serious, and you are involved in a breakup, try planting both a male and a female holly tree, side by side, someplace where you can attend to them. If you don't have a yard yourself, sponsor the trees in a friend's yard! As you plant them, place each of your names in the dug-out holes. Say a loving benediction, and tend the trees warmly.

THE SCENTS AND COLORS OF REBALANCE

Part of polarity magic is the ability to realize that a situation is under threat and to arrest it before it disappears irrevocably down a terminal path!

This may sound silly, but pause for a moment: if you can honestly assess a tricky relationship, or identify a potential cause of angry disagreement before it has deteriorated into intransigent behavior on both sides, you should be able to express disquiet or confusion without malice and insecurity, and avoid a serious problem. To achieve this equanimity, you need to breathe in the scents of balance, which effectively encourage you to try to see some of the problem from the other party's point of view. After all, the chances are that there are two sides to the quarrel or situation that has brought you to anger.

Surround yourself with a circle of eight candles, bronze-yellow in color, and with the use of an oil burner, breathe in tuberose oil, or benzoin, or geranium, or a mixture of the three. Ask yourself how a secure and balanced person, no longer in the first flush of wrath, would deal with this issue: can you find a steady, non-explosive way of framing your questions, and be reasonable about it? Once you have seen some way forward, take the scents with you to the meeting, or burn them while you are speaking to the other party on the telephone. A disaster could thereby be averted, and you will encourage the other person also to rebalance their viewpoint, and see the justness of your position.

If you are dealing with a person or people who are perpetually quick to anger, try sprinkling these rebalancing oils around the "arena" before you all meet. If an argument has already occurred and you need to patch things up, write the names of the parties involved on good-quality paper, saturate the page with one of the oils, and tie it into a little scroll secured with yellow ribbon and—if you can get it—gold sealing wax.

Send the mental message of peace and forgiveness with the act. Apologies will then be able to take place gently.

LETTING GO

Perhaps a quarrel has developed, and it is not the first time. The rebalancing that you have in mind is to release the anger and pain, and then to reverse your own feelings of emotion so that you can effectively move on. Consult chapter 6, on disenchantment, but work some of the following advice in with your magic.

Surround yourself with sunflowers, or use a mandrake if you can get one! Burn the oils of rebalance, and use a magnet to envision a reversal of the existing situation that has been making you unhappy. Now write your name on a piece of paper, and next to it write the name of the party who has caused you grief or distress. Tie up a holly leaf with the paper using yellow cord, and place the whole in a little plastic container. Cover with honey, then add a good pinch of salt. This shows a willingness to pour salt into the wound—but also to add honey which will heal it!

OTHER SYMBOLS YOU COULD UTILIZE FOR LETTING GO:

- A CLOCK RUNNING BACKWARD (to show time being reversed), and ribbons that are actually untied. Use these items with a photo either to let go yourself or to move the relationship back in time to the point of combustion. Then, re-imagine the ending you want as vividly as you can!

- A SEMICIRCLE (180 degrees), which is excellent for business magic. If money has been running out, pin a protractor to a dollar bill and tie with gold cord. Imagine everything running forward, healthy and positive.

Master Spell: To Reverse a Difficult Situation.

This spell will help you to turn back the clock—with either a situation you wish had never started, or one that may have started to deteriorate. It should erase negative feelings and insecurity.

You will need

A photo of the person with whom you have reached a stalemate, if relevant, or documents (such as a letter, note, lawsuit, or bank statement) that pertain to the impasse; a small mirror (no more than 8 x 10 in.) with a bronze or yellow frame; 8 sunshine-yellow votive candles; a small horseshoe-shaped magnet wrapped in yellow cord or ribbon; a large sunflower.

Moon phase: *Waning.*

Before you begin, focus for a very long time on the documents, or photo, and what they represent; try to think very calmly about the difficulty of the situation, but do not allow yourself to see it as irrevocable, even for a second.

Place the documents, or photo, on a table in front of the mirror, and light the candles. Breathe deeply, and be quiet and still. Retrace in your mind all the steps that led up to the current problem—but stop short of the actual disaster, quarrel, or let-down. If you can now perceive the one bad move that led to the present state of affairs, start to visualize strongly a large clockface, with the hands turning backward, and possibly even a calendar flipping back until you arrive at the day or hour when everything went wrong.

Now grasp the magnet in your hands, turn it toward the mirror and documents or photo, and draw in the light from the candle flames. Strongly envision the events immediately prior to the bad moment, and then vividly rewrite the outcome in your mind. Imagine that the conversation took a different direction, or that spiky words, or a negative reply, which came in place of something positive you had hoped for, are now replaced by a gentle, harmonious conclusion. Be bold in your mind, but avoid being pushy in what you wish to see occur; rather, see a gentle retraction of the negativity or unhappiness that occurred. See a much happier end to the whole episode. Focus on this thought, quietly, for several moments; imagine the face of the other person or people involved, and see yourself departing from them in a positive way. Circle them with light in your imagination; say *"sorry"* if necessary.

Loop the magnet into the documents or photo, and secure with yellow cord or ribbon. Place a sunny sunflower, symbol of hope, in front of the mirror where the papers or photo lay before—replacing sadness with brightness. Put the magnet and papers or photo into an envelope or box, and file them somewhere right away. Let the candles burn down in front of the mirror, and every so often revisit them, and imagine the happier conclusion again for a few minutes.

After no more than a week, if appropriate, reopen communications or contact the person—if they have not already approached you with the same goal in mind. If it is in your best interests, it should now be possible to repair the damage.

Variations on the Master Spell

If a business is busy but making no money,
a coin purse with the coins falling out (upside down) should be
juxtaposed with one facing upright with the money falling into
it. Use these symbols in front of the mirror, with the candle, then
continue as on page 107—imagining a healthier bank balance!

If you need to stop someone gossiping
about you—perhaps someone who is really causing you
damage—perform the spell exactly as on page 107, but place a
chain around the framed picture of the person doing the
gossiping, and use a small "luggage lock" to padlock it (if you do
not have a photo, write the person's name on a piece of paper,
then insert it into a photo frame and padlock the chain
around the frame). Imagine their destruction being locked off:
literally imagine their mouth "locked," unable to spread any more
calumny! Then, finish the spell as on page 107.

If you wish to stop someone's unhelpful
behavior, use yarrow, the herb of reversal, or camphor plant.
Tie either or both into a little yellow pouch and place it above a
mirror, or over the door. Then burn the candle in front of the
mirror, as on page 107.

)

IF A RELATIONSHIP IS BECOMING TOO HEAVY, or too sickly sweet, and you want to slow things up a little, immerse a small scroll with your names written on it into a pot of salt, and secure with bronze or yellow ribbon and sealing wax. Respectfully ask the other party to give you more leeway! Then burn the candle in front of the mirror, and send the mental message.

IF A BUSINESS OR OTHER RELATIONSHIP IS TOO POSSESSIVE, an open hand (as opposed to a tightly closed one) would be the symbol. Draw this, and rest your names on the open palm. Use this now as the "document" or "photo" in the master spell.

IF YOU WANT TO STOP SMOKING!—no easy task this, but envisioning your will as firm helps in fact to strengthen it; so, place a cigarette inside a padlock and put this in the center of the spell area as on page 107. Imagine that you are able to refuse the cigarette each time it is offered; burn the candle in front of the mirror *with* the padlocked cigarette, then adapt the remainder of the spell with the end in mind that you will always be able to refuse lighting a cigarette! This is self-hypnosis. Use the padlocked cigarette as your emblem, and place one in several different places to remind you of your decision to give up!

☽

This
CHAPTER IS CENTERED ON THE HAZEL MOON
—THE CRONE MOON, OR MOON OF THE WISE—AND TAKES
THE ACQUISITION OF KNOWLEDGE AND ALL MATTERS OF EDUCATION TO
ITS HEART. THIS IS THE MAGIC THAT WILL CONCERN ANYONE STUDYING,
TAKING AN EXAM, TRYING TO TAKE IN INFORMATION—OR EVEN ATTEMPTING TO GET A
POSITION AT AN EDUCATIONAL ESTABLISHMENT. WITHOUT BEING TOO GRAND, HOWEVER,
IT ALSO COVERS DRIVING TESTS (IN CONJUNCTION WITH THE ROWAN MOON OF TRAVEL—SEE
CHAPTER 2) AND COOKING COURSES! FROM EARLY AUGUST TO THE BEGINNING OF SEPTEMBER—

9 : WISDOM

THE PERIOD COVERED BY THE HAZEL MOON—WE
ARE WITNESSING THE LATE POWER OF THE SUN;
THIS IS A HEYDAY PERIOD: A MOMENT FOR REFLECTION AND HEIGHTENED AWARENESS. THERE IS
NO PARTICULAR CELEBRATION DAY WITHIN THIS MOON/MONTH. HOWEVER, WE CAN ENJOY A
PROLONGED HARVEST FESTIVAL RIGHT THROUGH THE PERIOD, FROM THE PREVIOUS HOLLY
MOON UNTIL THE VINE MOON OF CELEBRATION (IN CHAPTER 10); THIS COINCIDES WELL WITH
THE ENGLISH CHURCH'S HARVEST FESTIVAL. A "GOOD WITCH" STRIVES TO KNOW WHEN
IT IS VALID, AND WHEN INVALID, TO TACKLE ANY TASK IN MAGIC:
OR, PUT ANOTHER WAY, WHEN NOT TO DO OR UNDO SOMETHING. THERE
ARE ALWAYS TIMES WHEN IT IS BEST TO LEAVE WELL ENOUGH
ALONE—SOMETHING YOU WILL LEARN FROM
EXPERIENCE.

HAZEL MOON—MOON OF WISDOM. Colors: OLIVE GREEN, MULBERRY. Scents: HYACINTH, ROSE ATTAR (for forgiveness), ROSEMARY, SANDALWOOD, LAVENDER (for the mind). Number: 9. Now we set out to acquire wisdom.

"One impulse from a vernal wood
  May teach you more of man;
  Of moral evil and of good
  Than all the sages can."
"THE TABLES TURNED"
WILLIAM WORDSWORTH

This is a crucial element of this chapter. You have come thus far down the road, and are starting to grasp the mental elasticity required for good magic and to embrace very subtly the philosophy behind Wicca thinking. This is where you must now put your reflective powers into action, and make a difference—not only to your own life but also to those around you.

The hazel is the tree long held to be symbolic of the acquisition of knowledge and philosophy, but rather unusually, two other trees are associated with this moon cycle, owing to their long connection with wisdom, forgiveness, and spiritual understanding. The first of these is the mulberry, which refuses to put out any sign of growth until all danger of frost is past, and the second is the olive tree, which is sometimes one of the core thirteen trees, notably in the French Celtic tradition. The olive is, of course, associated with peace.

Hazel is one of the few witches' trees that were not valued primarily for their medicinal properties. Although it does have applications in medicine, its principal value comes from the use that can be made of its wood, its oil, and the nutritious nuts that it bears. The wood has long been used for walking sticks and rods (symbols of wisdom), as well as in the making of hurdle fences and wattles. Significantly, it is one of the main woods used to make divining rods (along with willow, or withy). Only someone wise, skilled, and patient could dowse—and indeed, to this day the job of diviner is often hereditary. Perhaps this is the first connection between the tree and wisdom.

Besides this, hazel nuts and oil are highly nutritious and might well be regarded as "brain food"—rich as they are in fat and protein. In the past, the oil was used not only in cooking (as now) but also to make soaps and cosmetics. In magic, this valuable oil is often used in ritual.

Mulberry is a byword for medicinal wisdom in China and has been cultivated for its beneficial properties since it was brought to Europe from the Middle East at the time of the Crusades. It is famously used as a food for silkworms, but the fruits are valued as diuretics and in the treatment of painful periods and diarrhea.

It is fascinating that the seventeenth-century herbalist Nicholas Culpeper lists both the hazel and the mulberry as ruled by Mercury, who is associated with wisdom and the hazel rod of knowledge. Inherent in this, the ninth moon, is the power of the number 9. This number embraces the philosophy of full knowledge; it is the last number of the ordinary cycle, 1 to 9, and assumes familiarity with all the numerological ideas that have passed before. As such it represents wisdom, forgiveness, wide reading, travel, and a humanitarian understanding of our fellow creatures—both human and animal.

THE MAGIC OF WISDOM IN EVERYDAY LIFE

The magic concerning wisdom is contemplative. It is important to recognize that we know very little straight off the top of our heads: or rather, whereas the initial impact of any given information will certainly touch off an intuitive response, it is the considered, well-rounded, patient conclusion we reach after some reflection that is the most reliable guide to our appropriate behavior and reaction in any situation. This moon reminds us not to "fly off the handle"; it exemplifies the pleasure and depth that come to us from learning and reading later in life, in place of the first rush of enthusiasm at best—and outright reluctance at worst—that we feel toward learning in the earlier part of our life. This moon is about the fruits of a little experience!

To turn up our capacity for receptiveness and open our minds to new information—instead of closing ourselves off to what is unfamiliar—certain colors, symbols, and scents spark off a more relaxed and inquiring state of mind. And here, for the first time as an essential, music plays a vital part in our developing brain. It is a belief seemingly common to all religious philosophy that "the music of the spheres" and chanting deepen our concentration and stimulate the mind to receive wisdom.

TRIGGERING MEMORY AND BRAIN ACTIVITY DAILY

- One way to step up your mental powers is to cover school books and work files in mulberry and/or olive colors, and scent the paperwork with a little of one of the oils listed on page 116. Or place scented handkerchiefs in your drawers, so that a little therapeutic aroma escapes as you work away, enticing your mind to stay fresh.

- Place a tissue imbued with the scents described on page 116, or a sachet of fresh rosemary and lavender, in your pencil case or disk box so that your mind is firing, but calmly, as you embark on work and education.

- Take a leaf out of a medieval book and strew herbs around your floor, or tie bunches around the study or office—again, make rosemary, lavender, and basil your principal choices.

- If you want to breathe in mental alertness—or an atmosphere of wise restraint—in the place where you work, grow one huge tub of herbs which includes rosemary, lavender, basil, and thyme, and even a small lemon tree if conditions allow. Stroking the leaves regularly, or before an important occasion, will release the right aromatic "buzz" into the room.

DOWSING

Begin on your path toward joining the adept by fashioning yourself a hazel rod (at last—a magic wand is prescribed!). Remember that it is symbolic of the tree of knowledge; if you can learn to use it to dowse, all the better.

Dowsers prefer to use the term "dowsing," instead of "divining," for this ancient method of discovering hidden substances under the earth. Hazel rods, cut in a fork shape, are the traditional tools for dowsing, though rowan wood and willow were also used; ash, too, had its place, and now metal rods, silk threads, and even nylon are used. Many farmers I have seen dowsing in the countryside where I live frown on any ceremony connected with the actual cutting of the hazel rods and simply cut the appropriate shape. So, if you want to try dowsing yourself—for water, treasure, minerals, or even archaeological finds—set about it thus:

Concentrate on what you are looking for, then grasp the two-pointed hazel rod by the ends of the fork with the bottom of the "Y" away from you. Walk gently (reflectively!) around the ground, and if you are properly attuned you will begin to receive transmissions from the object, or the water. Usually the rod begins to vibrate, and the end almost droops toward the source of energy.

This takes some practice; however, it is something that may make you feel closer to the earth's energies, and is worth bearing with until you have some success. If you can, learn at the feet of a master—try asking an experienced dowser to show you how to do it.

THE COLORS OF WISDOM AND FORGIVENESS

Green—the color of nature in full celebration—is associated with wisdom; the specific green, however, is not the emerald or the deep foresty green of the later reed moon (that of the home and hearth—see chapter 12); it is, instead, the olive green that comes from many ivies and trees of the autumn period. This color has the effect of slowing us down a little, and perhaps even inviting us to be grateful for the more subdued greens of the waning year. Mulberry is also in the spectrum of colors of wisdom, because it represents strength and vibrancy, but without aggressive energy. This was an expensive dye to extract in the Middle Ages, but was long lasting and much valued. In England, the Royal House of York used "murray" (a contraction of "mulberry") and blue as its colors.

A blending of the two represents reflection, calm, pensiveness, and mental activity and thought. They are my first choice for all of my files and stationery concerned with my study, and I burn candles in olive and mulberry when I am preparing for my exams to help me think through the work with clarity and to encourage my brain to work well!

If you want your brain ticking over well—but meditatively, perhaps, rather than creatively—buy yourself a present of a coffee mug in these hues, or tie ribbons around an existing favorite, and "breathe in" the colors. Let your thoughts run free, and allow your mind to achieve a particular level of concentration; play some gentle music to engage your mind still further. All this preparation is warranted before tackling important scholastic work, or reviewing for a test.

THE SCENTS OF WISDOM

Certain scents "switch on" the mind, enabling it to focus more easily and aiding our mental alertness. The acquisition of knowledge—and wisdom—is largely about making the best use of our very considerable mental capabilities. If we think of our brain as the most elaborate computer ever created and realize how lost we are with a brand new PC that is more sophisticated than one we've been used to unless we have time and clear instructions on how to use it, then we may be able to grasp just how little we really know about the potential of our minds.

If we can focus clearly on any task—that is, direct all our energy and attention to the issue at hand—we will achieve greater results for our efforts. Those who focus properly come at the top of their class, whatever that "class" is. They remember things better, and they understand the myriad ramifications of and interconnections between related areas. There are clearly some scents that push our brains into greater mental alertness, and harnessing these is a great aid to acquiring wisdom and knowledge.

Just to get your mind engaged in daily tasks that require concentration (especially study), inhale a few drops of rosemary and lemon essential oils on a tissue, or in a burner. Using a scented tissue is an easy way to renew concentration and clarity if you are taking an exam or going for an interview at which you must show mental dexterity and a familiarity with many points.

If you are preparing for an exam, presentation, or lecture, try adding lemon, rosemary, and lavender oils to your bath, and really clearing your mind as you breathe in the steamy concoction. If you have to prepare for something completely new, select a blend of oils that make a rather unusual choice, so that you don't cloud your mind with memories connected with other things as well. Scent definitely triggers memories—and you want to use this to your advantage, not to cause an overload! Other oils you can choose that stimulate the mind and help you to focus and think clearly are basil, bergamot, ginger, and grapefruit, so make up your own blend and stick to the formula until the job is finished.

THE SYMBOLS OF WISDOM. Remember that knowledge alone is not wisdom: wisdom is the ability to turn knowledge into sound behavior, to be guided toward a beneficial outcome for you and those around you. Even in a love relationship, one may have knowledge of certain truths about the loved one, but it will require wisdom to know how to deal with these facts to ensure the smooth flow of the relationship. WISDOM IS BEYOND KNOWLEDGE.

Meditating on, and incorporating into your life, any of the following symbols should serve as a reminder to think through the ultimate ramifications of all you do. In magic, awareness is the key: to be aware that every action has a connected reaction is an important truth. Always think ahead to what the repercussions may be, instead of acting hastily.

OWLS, BOOKS, SCROLLS, STYLUS, AND PAPER are all symbolic of learning, and magic ritual to encourage daily use of your wisest faculties should draw on some of these emblems. If you are preparing important work, or studying, or beginning a new college life, burn a candle on the eve of your new adventure and find one of these symbols (even in a picture) to rest beside your name, underneath the candle. The candle should be olive green or mulberry in color and could be scented with one of the oils listed on page 116. You should ask for a blessing on your venture: ask that your senses remain strongly with you, and that wise behavior attend your actions and inform your moves.

A HAZEL STAFF (or divining rod) has already been mentioned on page 116: dowse for relaxation and focused thought before an important mental challenge. Equally, adding hazelnuts and hazelnut oils to your diet will act as brain food, and as a reminder that you should act with serene wisdom in your daily endeavors. Incorporate the symbols (or strew the nuts) around your work space for their magical properties.

The most potent magical symbol for luck in gaining knowledge and achieving wisdom is the MULBERRY TREE. I use a mulberry leaf, twig, or berry in any magic required for wise meditation. Even before deciding what course of action to take, I burn a candle and meditate on a mulberry leaf to ask for guidance. As a child, I was fonder of the fragrant mulberry tree than of any other in the garden. Mulberries are still the taste of my happy childhood, reminding me to be happy in the simplest of things.

TAROT IX, the Wise Hermit, is a powerful symbol in the magic of learning. Make yourself a talisman for a fortuitous start to a new education, or job concerned with education, using this card. You might make yourself a cushion for your study chair or work seat, comprising your own name, a benediction for learning, and the symbol of TAROT ARCANUM IX. As you make it, think of being a proponent of the wisdom of the centuries: think of being unhurried in decision, and just in arriving at a course of action. Stuff the pillow with herbs related to mental agility: rosemary, of course, and lavender, basil, thyme, even lemon peel.

A BOTTLE OF "WITCH-HAZEL," AN HOURGLASS (wisdom is concerned very much with patience), A SNAKE, SERPENT, OR DRAGON, AND A SNAIL (again for patience) are all concerned with acquiring wisdom. An olive branch, or tree, will remind you of the constant need for forgiveness. A wise soul knows how important all these attributes are and how far to temper one's actions with kindness and understanding. This, of course, does not always mean giving in to another's plans or wishes. When you need to be strong, to stand by a decision you have made that you know is wise, even in the face of pressure (emotional blackmail, perhaps), surround yourself with any of these emblems of great power, burn a candle, inhale the scents of the mind, and stick serenely to your cause.

All the magic of wisdom draws on the elements of heightened senses: the ear to the ground, listening for the secrets of the earth; the nose in the wind, detecting scent and movement; the sight applied to clouds, earth, and trees, for signs of change; the tongue still—so that you listen, instead of talking. Draw on these images as part of your everyday magic-making to learn to be adept. Remember that speech is silver, but silence is golden.

MASTER SPELL 1: TO AID IN ABSORBING KNOWLEDGE. This master spell is designed to intensify your mental powers and prepare you to take on any knowledge with serenity and confidence. With minor adaptations, it will work just as well for someone taking their driving test as for someone facing exams.

YOU WILL NEED
An hourglass; 1 large off-white church candle infused with rosemary oil; some music you enjoy relaxing to; about 1 yard of olive green or mulberry ribbon; beautiful paper on which to write a personal pledge; an olive-green velvet pouch; 9 hazelnuts.

MOON PHASE: *Any, but especially full.*

Begin the spell by turning up your hourglass and watching the sands drift through it for a moment. The whole spell should unfold over the duration of the hourglass's emptying. Pledge to be patient in life—to allow good things in you to distill properly.

Light your candle and put on some soft, classical, or instrumental music that helps you to feel relaxed and peaceful, but at the same time thoughtful. Bind the ribbon around your brow, and imagine your brain feeling receptive, flexible, and hungry for knowledge. Imagine the candlelight and the ribbon penetrating the dark corners of your mind, illuminating it with knowledge and information, and imagine your brain becoming more alive. See if you can picture more of your brain actually being engaged. Vividly see a further sector of your mind waking up, ready to take on new facts and discover more capacity. Close your eyes and concentrate on what lies ahead: if you are studying, pause to consider the material you need to be familiar with; if you are about to take a test, sweep gently over the subject in a kind of video montage that recalls highlights of it. Open

your eyes and look at the candle. Be determined: see yourself successful in the hours from now right through to completion of your important task.

Write on the paper a pledge to be more receptive to new facts and aware of broader issues—to listen and learn more. In your own words, pledge not to be "closed" to any information or subject; promise to spend time actively gleaning more from life—of people's characters, make-up, and psychological disposition, as well as of history, literature, technology, or whatever else fascinates you. Sign the paper and date it; finish with a postscript asking for success in the venture ahead, or whatever situation has inclined you to cast this spell (you could write simply, *exam luck* or something similar). Put the paper in the velvet pouch with the hazelnuts. Do not hurry these actions.

Inhale the light, the scent, the music, and think again about the subject that has prompted your magic; if it is a test or exam, or the presentation of a lecture, speech, or other material, think—while looking at the candle flame and smelling the rosemary—about the information you are required to retain. Say some of the key things out loud.

Let the candle burn down for the remainder of the hour. Finally, unbind the ribbon from your brow and tie the pouch closed with it. Take it with you to your exam, or whatever the occasion may be.

MASTER SPELL 11: TO HEIGHTEN YOUR SENSES. This spell is not about acquiring knowledge, but about preparing your senses to perform at their peak—whether for learning, thinking, socializing, or any other situation where peak performance is required.

YOU WILL NEED

A talisman made of silver or gold: choose a deer, a hare, or a rabbit, or, if you prefer, a dog, cat, or horse; a handful of herbs and fresh flowers for crushing to release their fragrance; a short length of mulberry-colored ribbon.

MOON PHASE: *Any.*

Choose a bright early morning, preferably when the sun is just rising and the moon is still up. If you are a city dweller, go to a park or a stretch of clear, green land; if you live in the country, make the most of a tranquil setting. Hold up your talisman—first to the moon before she sets, and then to the sun as he rises. This could be a silver or gold brooch, a charm of one of the animals above, or possibly a little ceramic or glass figure if this is all you can find. The animals listed symbolize the most alert and still qualities in the animal kingdom; the hare, in particular, is a special favorite for this because it is the messenger of the moon and thought to be one of the shapes assumed by a witch if she has to disappear because of danger.

Ask for the secrets of day and night; ask for a oneness with the creation; ask for special powers to see without always being seen, to hear without always being heard, to smell without being smelled.

Now sit and gently crush some of the herbs and flowers, one at a time, in your hand, releasing their aroma. Good choices are early violets, primroses, jonquils, dianthus, and any of the herbs available at the time. The most appropriate is one that is quite subtly scented. Encourage your senses to open completely and take on the feel, look, and fragrance of every individual plant. Make sure you could recognize it again with your eyes blindfolded! Know it by feel as well as by smell. Do this with each herb/flower.

Now put your ear to the earth, and listen. Close your eyes, and listen to the sounds of the earth stirring: birds, distant traffic, crunching twigs, and moving branches. Listen until sounds you never normally bother to pick out emerge with such clarity that you can almost hear the electricity wires humming, or someone's kettle singing! You might hear your own breath, your heart, even your watch ticking.

Look at everything with new eyes: take in the exact color of the sky; the trees in early light; the ground moist with dew; the precise hue of your sweater, or even your skin, in the morning light. Now offer up your animal talisman again to the moon and sun, and quietly walk home, trying hard not to be heard, but listening to everything, looking at everything, smelling all the scents on the way back. Remember the exquisite sensations, and vow to carry these with you more often—to train your senses to brim with awareness and feeling.

Carry your talisman, tied with the ribbon, whenever you need your senses to be most alive.

THIS

CHAPTER EMBRACES THE VINE MOON—THE

MOON OF CELEBRATION—WHICH FALLS AT THE MOMENT OF

THE RIPE HARVEST. THIS IS THE AUTUMN EQUINOX (CALLED MABON,

THE FERTILE PRINCIPLE IN CELTIC MYTH) AND IS A MOMENT OF UNABASHED

JOY. WE LOOK AT RECIPES FOR FEASTING DERIVED FROM TRADITIONAL CELTIC

AND CORNISH CUSTOM, AND WILL SEE HOW WE CAN SLIP "MAGIC" INGREDIENTS INTO

EVERYDAY FOOD TO ACHIEVE A POWERFUL, ENCHANTING HOLD ON LIFE AND BUOY UP

THE SPIRITS OF EVERYONE AROUND US—BUT AS EVER, WE MUST DO THIS WITH INTEGRITY.

10:CELEBRATION

RECIPES ARE GIVEN FOR FLOWER AND

HERB-FLAVORED DISHES, AND FOR FEAST WINES, WHICH WERE ALWAYS AT THE HEART OF THE

CELEBRATIONS ASSOCIATED WITH THE TIME OF THE VINE MOON—THE NICEST OF THESE IS THE

CHAMPAGNE COCKTAIL, WHICH HAS A LEMONY FLAVOR AND STRONGLY APHRODISIAC EFFECT. THIS

MOON ALSO GOVERNS "BINDING SPELLS," WHICH USE THE VINE TO BIND ANY SITUATION,

FROM MARRIAGE TO A RELATIONSHIP THAT IS THREATENING TO BREAK UP. COVERING

THE MONTH OF SEPTEMBER, THIS MOON AND MOMENT ARE THE BEST EXCUSE ALL

YEAR TO LET YOUR HAIR DOWN AND APPRECIATE THE NATURAL RHYTHMS

OF THE EARTH'S CYCLES, OUR PART IN WORKING WITH THEM,

AND THE BOUNTY THIS HAPPIEST OF MARRIAGES

YIELDS TO US.

VINE MOON—MOON OF CELEBRATION AND HARVEST. Colors: SILVER, BURGUNDY. Scents: EUCALYPTUS, BENZOIN, MANDARIN. Number: 10. The vine is the active symbol of work well rewarded. As such, it might be an emblem of what we hope for in life: the combination of a wise marriage with nature, diligence regarding our duty, a little luck from above, and a well-earned culmination in festivity following work completed.

"And still she slept an azure-lidded sleep,
In blanched linen, smooth, and lavender'd,
While he from forth the closet brought a heap
Of candied apple, quince, and plum, and gourd;
With jellies smoother than the creamy curd,
And lucent syrops, tinct with cinnamon;
Manna and dates, in argosy transferr'd
From Fez; and spiced dainties, every one,
From silken Samarcand to cedar'd Lebanon."
"THE EVE OF ST AGNES"
JOHN KEATS

In magic, the vine is a potent symbol. The passion vine is religious, exotic, resilient. Blueberry and blackberry vines stand for protection and resilience; grapevines further suggest prosperity and a dream link with the past. Hops are connected with healing. All the vines can be used in magic spells for binding—as in a contract, an agreement between people, a love relationship that is becoming more serious or indeed threatening to break away—and to bless children or loved ones as they must go away from you.

The main purpose of the vine moon in the magical calendar, however, concerns justified feasting and joyous thanksgiving. This, then, is largely a cooking chapter, and it will also demonstrate ways of showing a festive spirit in everyday life—or how to make magic in any celebratory situation. It reminds us of the need for enthusing in life—of spreading warmth and happiness, of helping ourselves and others to balance duty and pressure with outright merriment.

The symbols of the magic celebration are mostly foods associated with harvest, for in this period of the year there are variations on harvest festivals from late September through October (embracing Halloween), right up to Thanksgiving in November.

The colors are also associated with the ripening vines. In the early moist, even frosty, mornings, heavy dew brings a silvery sheen to the vines, and the deep burgundy color of the grapes is sometimes matched by the dark reddish hue of the leaves touched by light frost. These, then, are the colors of ripeness: they have a surreal effect on the senses, and used magically, they inject *joie de vivre* into our being.

Here, we will perform the ceremony of cakes and ale—almost an altar to feasting. We will brew an ale, but also make a champagne cocktail—a townies' wine, in case you think the cider ale sounds a bit countrified. We will also make gardenia, lavender, and rose ice creams and send all our friends ribbon-tied cards to celebrate life.

SPREADING EUPHORIA

Now we send magic everywhere by hanging bunches of ribbons, flowers, and pendulous ornaments; this is the moment of "festooning." All the colors used up to date should be tied, rainbow style, around the life you lead in September.

Oils for burning are eucalyptus, melissa, lavender, benzoin, and mandarin. Send cards to friends written with perfumed ink (adding three or four drops of sandalwood, rose attar, neroli, or bergamot to the ink pot and shaking well: all these oils are for joy), tied around the middle with a rainbow of colored ribbons and spattered with a drop or two of one of these oils. Send a prayer for their good fortune and happiness before you seal the envelope—which you could also cram with a few heavily scented rose petals.

Bake simple cakes covered with thick whipped cream and then strewn with late rose petals. Take them to friends who have been feeling a bit down; ask them to "make a wish" (an old Pagan cakes-and-ale prayer if ever there was one) as they cut the cake and to believe in its power to bring the wish home. Invite other friends to afternoon teas and serve the meal with whipped cream and rose petals. Beautiful late sunsets will make a perfect backdrop to wishing magic shared in celebratory teas with friends. Offer unusual teas made from gardenia or borage flowers, or jasmine if you still have some blooming: all three lift the spirits and are beloved of the gods.

Wine in beautiful glassware to share with many friends is another beautiful vine moon custom: the glasses must be the best you can afford, glinting in the late sun/early moon. Use the champagne cocktail, or the ale described on pages 130–1. FEASTING. JOY.

CELEBRATION MAGIC IN EVERYDAY LIFE

- Give small nosegays of flowers to people who look sad or stressed.

- Pot up autumn seeds for friends, with "wishes" (written on tiny bits of paper) "sown" into the soil.

- Fill your car with a rainbow of balloons and take a friend driving into the country to watch a late sunset.

- Make a floral wreath on your door as though it were Christmas, weaving colored ribbons, grapes, and late flowers into it. Wish for joy as you work, then ask friends around for dinner.

- Wear colorful clothes deliberately to spread color from your footsteps everywhere you go.

MAGIC IN FOOD. The idea of food magic is that certain substances inherent in herbs and flowers, when combined in particular ways, alter our perception or state of being for a while. Now that we have been able to test the properties of herbs more effectively, we can understand the claim better than before; for it is certainly true that the complex chemicals in herbs, which are natural rather than synthesized, have a direct impact on our health and well-being. The age-old tradition, then, is to incorporate these "magical ingredients" into our menu.

WITCHES' BREAD

I have no idea whether this recipe is known to other Wiccans, but my grandmother used to make it and always called it "witches' bread." Perhaps it was partly self-mocking. However, from what I can tell, it is very close to the recipe for soda bread—with a few herbs added for magic and flavor. It is very easy to make and does not require any yeast.

The herbs used vary, but a combination of marjoram and rosemary was always at the center of it: the former seems to have a tonic effect and can also help to counteract irritability, while the latter, being antiseptic, helps to preserve foods but also stimulates the brain and seems to have a beneficial effect on our cholesterol count. The other herb my grandmother used was calendula (marigold), or if available, wild chrysanthemum. The first is known as an antidepressant, and the second was believed to bestow long life. Indeed, it now seems it may have anti-cancer properties. Consume this bread, then, for a long and healthy life, active mind, and the ability to cope with stress. It should be broken apart, not cut.

When eaten with friends, the bread will form the center of a simple but delicious feast with both physical and spiritual properties.

YOU WILL NEED

2 cups of white flour; 2 cups of wholewheat flour; a pinch of salt; 2 teaspoons of baking soda; 2 teaspoons of baking powder; 31/2 tablespoons of butter (lard was traditional); 3 tablespoons of oatmeal; fresh herbs (as opposite); a small beaten egg; 17 fl. oz. of buttermilk (or milk soured with vinegar and lemon juice).

Sift together the flours, salt, baking soda, and baking powder, then cut or rub in the butter and oatmeal so that the mixture resembles fine breadcrumbs. Toss the finely cut herbs through the mixture. Make a well in the center of the bowl, and add the beaten egg and buttermilk, using a knife to combine the ingredients. Knead very lightly against the sides of the bowl, then shape into two rounds—like cakes. Put them into well-greased 8 in. round pans, and cut a cross into the top of the bread right across the diameter, so that you effectively mark out four quarters. Dust the top lightly with flour, or brush with a little milk. Bake for about 30–35 mins at 400°F. Turn out onto a wire rack to cool.

THE ICE CREAMS

Ice cream was formerly a luxury at the end of a meal. The old method of making it required access to an ice house, an elaborate wooden bucket with a spindle for churning, and the use of salt to boost the cooling effect of the ice. All in all, it was a special achievement to make ice cream—which we have forgotten, because of the ease of doing so now with modern ice-cream makers.

The addition of the exotic flowers—lavender, gardenia, and rose—intensified the exotic quality of the ice cream itself; but besides providing flavor and fragrance, the flowers have potent magical properties which affect the one who consumes it deliciously.

- LAVENDER eases away aches, headache, nausea, and tiredness—which makes it a restorative for the end of a meal or long feast (or even a long day at the office). It is also widely regarded as an aphrodisiac—perhaps simply because of the qualities already mentioned, and the fact that it counters bad breath.

- ROSE reputedly also has great powers to counter unpleasant breath; it has a long history of use medicinally as well as in culinary and cosmetic preparations. The scent cheers the senses and may have a calming effect on the heart, while the petals—made into a tea and used in cooking—are an excellent tonic for those who are convalescing or run down. The petals are also traditionally used in the treatment of stress and anxiety—which may account for their use in magical cookery.

- GARDENIA is the most exotic of the three, and is the most magical in the imagination of the witch working love recipes. Perhaps it is the intensely sweet fragrance; and even today,

in Chinese medicine the flowers and fruits are acknowledged to lift the spirits, and be inspirational.

A Trio of Ice Creams

These ice creams are especially easy to prepare. They are all made without the aid of an ice-cream maker, relying instead on alcohol to raise the temperature at which the mixture freezes and prevent ice crystals from forming. There is no need to whip the mixture at intervals.

You will need

2 large gardenia flowers; 3 or 4 fragrant roses—gallica or damask types are best; several sprigs of lavender flowers (preferably fresh, or dried if necessary); 3 x 1/3 cup of superfine sugar; 3 x 6 large eggs, separated; 3 x 11/4 pt. of heavy cream; 3 x 1 fl. oz. of cognac or kirsch.

For each ice cream, infuse the flowers individually in an airtight jar with the sugar for three or four days, shaking gently each day. Over these few days the flavors will develop in each jar of sugar.

Make each mixture separately. For each of the three ice creams, grease a large charlotte or gelatin mold thoroughly. Set the flowers aside and beat the individual sets of egg yolks with each of the sugars until each mixture is pale and fluffy. Now whip the cream and incorporate the flowers as you beat it until thick. (For the gardenia, it is best to tear the flower petals to release the remaining fragrance before adding them to the cream.) Fold each of the creams into each of the egg mixtures.

Now beat each set of whites in a chilled bowl until very stiff peaks form. Fold the whites gently into the other mixtures with a metal spoon, and add the alcohol now. You can add extra petals from the individual flowers if you want more texture in the ice creams—but don't overdo it. Add a few drops of lemon juice to deepen the lavender color of the lavender ice cream; a few drops of glycerine added to the rose will deepen its color a little too.

Pour each individual mixture into one of the molds, and cover with plastic wrap. Freeze for at least 6–8 hours, or overnight, to let the flavors intensify. Unmold by immersing the mold in very hot water for a few seconds, and turn each ice cream onto a serving plate. They can be decorated casually with fresh flowers and—for the gardenia—leaves, and served immediately.

These ice creams make a literally magical end to any ordinary dinner: save them for someone you really love, to create a mood of ease and abundant good humor.

Cakes and Ale

The center of any harvest festival is bread, but the idea that consuming food made the matter it consisted of live again—and that the symbolic connection between the food and a corporal idea was borne aloft by eating it, as in the Christian ceremony of Holy Communion—is behind the ritual of cakes and ale.

Cakes and ale form the apogee of a celebratory feast: this is the completion of the cycle of spirit and transcendent being. The cake is representative of the material world; the ale is the spirit of fire and air, as well as water. Both are usually dedicated to the deities, and again, the rite of eating the food signifies taking on divine strength and grace within the individual or the company.

Always bless your bread, and ask that it return manifold. For this reason, the rite of cakes and ale is largely concerned with health, prosperity, and fertility.

SIMPLE CELEBRATION CAKE

This recipe is fairly typical of several Cornish, and indeed Breton, special afternoon cakes. It is a simple cake but very moist, and tastes delicious straight from the oven: but the secret ingredient is the rose geranium—sometimes, apple geranium is substituted.

The effect of this herb is to flavor the cake subtly and make something delicate and ethereal out of it, while at the same time the antidepressant properties of the herb seem literally to lift our spirits and make us more inclined to put our cares away and feel positive.

YOU WILL NEED

11/2 cups of flour; 1/4 teaspoon of baking powder; 3 large eggs; 3/4 cup of melted butter; 3/4 cup of white sugar; 2 tablespoons of kirsch or brandy; 4 or 5 rose geranium leaves, torn apart loosely (if you use cider brandy, use apple geranium leaves instead); extra geranium leaves or flowers to garnish.

Sift the flour and baking powder into a bowl and mix in the eggs with a wooden spoon, then add the butter, sugar, and kirsch or brandy. Once the mixture has a smooth consistency, add the geranium leaves. The mixture should be relatively liquid.

Butter a medium-sized cake pan and line it with waxed paper or baking parchment. Pour the mixture into the pan and bake at 400°F for 25–30 minutes. Let the cake cool, then turn out and decorate with geranium leaves or flowers.

Consume the cake while it is still warm—"blood temperature"—and dedicate a slice of it to the gods. Afterward, crumble that slice for the birds, or over the soil. The cake has a definite impact on the senses, and will lift your spirits even if you have had a stressful day. Thus, if you partake of it with a lover, you will feel more sanguine and sprightly together.

CHAMPAGNE COCKTAIL—A LOVE POTION

The most celebratory drink I know of is a guaranteed magic draft. Borage is one of the witch's most magic plants, for it cheers the senses utterly. This seems to be because it stimulates the production of adrenalin, and it has a long association as the herb of euphoria. Put into ice cubes, it makes a wonderful garnish for any summer drink. It has the magic power in champagne to intoxicate the senses and entice another being to think wonderfully of you—use wisely. First make a syrup . . .

YOU WILL NEED

2 or 3 borage leaves, and the same number of flowers; 2 tablespoons of sugar or honey; 1/2 cup of water; juice of 1 lemon; a sugar cube; one or two drops of Angostura bitters; a small shot of good brandy; champagne; 1–2 extra borage flowers to garnish.

Bring the first four ingredients gently to the boil while dissolving the sugar in the liquid, and reduce until a thick syrup is produced. Chill thoroughly.

Saturate a sugar cube with the syrup in the bottom of a flute glass, add the bitters and the brandy, then top with good champagne. Add one or two more flowers for garnish. Share with your lover and leave all your cares behind...BLISS!

THE ALE

A traditional English West Country ale for special occasions is effectively an apple cider punch—which uses plenty of hedgerow produce to give it an extra kick. The key is to infuse the gin with the sloes and subsequently absorb all the tonic properties of this beautiful blue-black fruit from the blackthorn tree. The wonderful pinky color it creates with the gin is guaranteed to lift the spirits anyway—but do not drive afterward. The longer you let the sloe gin mature, the more delicious and potent the properties of the drink—a year is not too long. To half a bottle of gin add 3/8 cup of sugar, 3 1/2 cups of sloes, 1 cup of whole almonds, and a teaspoon of brandy for flavor. Macerate the almonds, or bruise them, slit the sloes open with a sharp knife, and bottle the nuts and fruit with the brandy, sugar, and gin. Seal the bottle, and shake well each day for at least two weeks. Store it away from the light for a month minimum.

Then, to make the ale…

You will need
2 quarts of cider; sloe gin (as above); 1 cup of sherry (or rum); 2 lemons; 2 oranges; 3 tablespoons of sugar; plenty of fresh lemon balm and mint leaves; chilled mineral water.

Carefully combine the three alcoholic beverages in a large punch bowl; slice the citrus fruits, peels intact, and add to the mixture with the sugar. Crush the lemon balm and mint, add to the bowl, chill, and dilute with sparkling mineral water to serve. Wow!

The ale and either the bread or cake can now be used to toast the spirit of prosperity and long life, as well as offering to the deity. The server should pass the bread and drink to the left (in other words, clockwise), as it is bad luck to go "widdershins"(or counterclockwise) for a celebratory rite. Always return some of the cakes and ale to the earth at the conclusion of the feasting.

Remember to serve your drink in vessels tied with burgundy or silver ribbon (or both), and to make a wish for general prosperity and health as you do so. Remember, too, to give thanks for all the blessings you receive in your life.

MASTER SPELL: TO ENSURE THE SUCCESS OF A PARTY OR SPECIAL EVENT.

This spell is designed for all guests to share in at a special occasion: it will suit any, so there are few variations. The vines are present to "bind" the joy to the spell participants, and are appropriate whether you are celebrating a wedding, naming day or christening, graduation, birthday, anniversary, housewarming, new job—in fact absolutely anything. The goal, of course, is to continue the joy from this day on, ad infinitum...

YOU WILL NEED
Vines; 1 yard each of silver and burgundy ribbon; a clean white (or cream) pillar candle; name(s) of the person or people whom the celebration honors, written on a small piece of paper with perfumed ink; several needles; silver and burgundy balloons (any quantity), into which silver stars have been inserted.

MOON PHASE: *Any, but waxing would be good.*

Decorate the venue with some vines: include passion vine if you can get it, otherwise grape and ivy are lovely.

Before the main festivities are under way, tape out the ribbon into a pentagram star (five points). Use both colors, and lay one over the other. Place the candle in the middle, with the name(s) of the person or people concerned on paper underneath the candle. Ask the participants to join·in the wish.

The spell will now be "formed" when all the guests join in the toast and, taking a needle warmed at the candle in the stars, burst the balloons so that the stars descend on the speller or couple or—numbers permitting—all the guests as well. The principal person or people honored should take home a piece of the vine, twined around the left arm, to bind the joy of this occasion to them prosperously, now and in the future.

VARIATIONS ON THE MASTER SPELL

IF THE CELEBRATION IS FOR A WEDDING,
put some confetti and some orange blossom fragrance into the balloons, along with the stars. When they burst, the room will have a magical orange scent—which is lucky for weddings.

IF THE OCCASION IS A CHRISTENING OR NAME-DAY,
choose rose petals and fragrance for a girl, dried herbs and citrus notes for a boy, and do the same as for the variation above.

☽

We

NOW REACH THE TOPICS OF HEALTH, VITALITY

AND BEAUTY. WE EXAMINE RESILIENCE TO THE ELEMENTS,

TO MOOD TESTS, TO LOVE TRIALS: RESILIENCE IS THE KEY TO SURVIVING

ALL OF LIFE'S TESTS. IVY IS BELOVED MAGICALLY FOR ITS TENACITY, ITS

RESILIENCE AND ITS BEAUTY. THE IVY MOON — WHICH COVERS THE PERIOD FROM THE

END OF SEPTEMBER TO LATE OCTOBER — IS ALSO THE MOON OF BUOYANCY: THIS CONCERNS

OUR CAPACITY TO SEE THE BEST IN EVERYTHING AND KEEP OUR SPIRITS HIGH AT ALL TIMES.

THE ESSENCE OF THIS CHAPTER IS HEALTH, AND ALL MAGIC RELATES EITHER TO REMAINING

11:RESILIENCE

HEALTHY AND BEAUTIFUL, OR TO RECOVERING HEALTH BEFORE

WE ARE IN TRUE CRISIS. THIS INCLUDES MENTAL HEALTH — DEPRESSION — AND WE LOOK FOR

MAGICAL WAYS TO BOOST OUR PSYCHOLOGICAL STATE WHEN WE ARE UNDER SIEGE. THE COLOURS

AND SCENTS FOR HEALTH ARE LOOKED AT; BUT MOST IMPORTANTLY, A 'MAGIC DIET' IS INCLUDED,

WHICH EXAMINES HERBS FOR EVERYDAY HEALTH AND MENTAL WELL-BEING. A WITCH'S

HERB LORE WAS WHAT TRADITIONALLY DISTINGUISHED HER AS A WITCH. THE MONTH

COVERED BY THE IVY MOON IS PERHAPS THE MOST FECUND AND RESILIENT TIME

IN NATURE, WHEN THE LAST HEADY DAYS OF AUTUMN SUNSHINE

PROLONG THE BEAUTY OF THE SEASON BEFORE THE ONSET

OF WINTER. IT IS A CELEBRATION OF HEALTHY

MATURITY.

IVY MOON—MOON OF RESILIENCE AND BUOYANCY. Colors: DEEP FOREST-GREEN, BLACK. Scents: ROMAN CHAMOMILE, LAVENDER, GRAPEFRUIT, PEPPERMINT, HYACINTH, MARJORAM, JASMINE, PATCHOULI, ORRIS, SANDALWOOD, ROSEWOOD (the "rainbow of scent"). Number: 11 (the master number).

"Season of mists and mellow fruitfulness.
Close bosom-friend of the maturing sun:
Conspiring with him how to load and bless
With fruit the vines that round the thatch-eaves run."
"TO AUTUMN"
JOHN KEATS

Once ivy is firmly established in any garden it is very difficult to eradicate, and from September to November, in northern climes, it produces wonderful clusters of yellow-green flowers at a time when most other garden plants are dying back. It clings determinedly to old ruined walls and derelict houses; it scrambles over forgotten paths and clothes fallen tree trunks with a new form of life which becomes a haven for other living things.

Since ancient times the ivy's magical powers have been renowned: as the "enemy of the vine," it has a long association with defeating intoxication, and it is connected with the treatment of headache and migraine. However, it is quite poisonous if strong doses are taken internally, and only the expressed juice is now used as an external compress for aching limbs, swollen feet, and cellulitis, so do not treat yourself with this herb except on professional medical advice.

Ivy is used symbolically in magic, for its tenacity and ability to cling; it is a symbol of good health, as it grows to a ripe age and beautifies during the barren months. The plant stands for optimism; it asks us to believe that good must ultimately prevail no matter how testing life becomes. When all else is bare, the fingers of green ivy add color and vivacity to naked trees and soil. We should dig deep and breathe in the delicious herby smell of the life around us. We should cling on. WE SHOULD BE AS RESILIENT AS THE IVY—WHICH SEEMS ABLE TO STAND EVEN THE SEVEREST FROST.

If you have been feeling downhearted or under the weather and tired out, surround yourself with magic images of resilience in the form of rubber and elastic. In everyday magic spells, rubber bands can be used to suggest the capacity to bounce back. Describe a five-pointed star in forest-green ribbon, place your picture in the middle, and put a lovely bouncy rubber ball (tiny and colorful) on top. Pick it up for a few minutes each day and bounce it on the floor, seeing your own face bouncing back into glowing health and rejuvenated action.

THE WITCH'S HERBALL, OR THE DIET OF EVERYDAY MAGICAL HEALTH.

The selection of lettuces in the supermarket is now so varied that it hardly seems necessary to describe the need for a varied herbal diet to maintain health. However, our ancestors had little access to such a wealth of natural vitamins, and a diet enriched with herbs was often the difference between sickness and health. So, advice on this subject was perhaps the most valuable a witch could give.

The following herbs formed the nucleus of the witch's garden and were prescribed for health and their magical properties. Undoubtedly, if you vary your diet to include many of them regularly, you will maintain strength and good spirits and rarely be on the sick list, while herbs that help to keep you calm must allay many problems. If you have little space to grow them yourself, many of these herbs are available fresh, either potted or flat-packed, in supermarkets.

SAGE There is an old proverb that runs, *"Why should a man die, who has sage in his garden?"* This herb was the most essential in preserving (and even, it was thought, creating) life. A general tonic for both mind and body, it is highly regarded for its digestive properties—which is why it is a famous accompaniment for fatty meats such as duck, pork, and even lamb—while also being a tonic for the nerves and stimulating to the circulation. This makes it an ideal tea for anyone suffering from stress or exhaustion, and it is wonderful for those who are convalescing. Red (or purple) sage is the correct choice for throat inflammations, but use garden sage plentifully in cooking to keep in good health and promote an efficient working system. Make a strong decoction of the herb (1/2 oz. of dried, or ten fresh, sage leaves steeped in boiling water for ten minutes) to combat skin irritations. This is the most important herb in the witch's medicine cabinet.

CLARY This is another herb that aids digestion, and it adds a delicious flavor to salads and cooked vegetable dishes. Use only a tiny amount. Added to wine or beer it intensifies the flavor but also has the power to lift the spirits of the imbiber. Definitely worth growing a little—or at least burning the essential oil when you're feeling stretched.

ANGELICA This well-known cake decoration had, in the past, a much more distinguished reputation than we accord it nowadays. Both a stimulant and a tonic herb, grated angelica root was made into a tea (1/2 oz. of grated root—somewhat like ginger—added to a quart of boiling water, steeped for a quarter of an hour) and consumed if the spirits were low or someone was lethargic. Do not do this too often, or it will prove more stimulating than coffee.

BORAGE My own favorite for cheering up even the most unpromising day. Make a decoction as a healthy tea (1 oz. in a quart of boiling water, boiled for another minute, then steeped for another ten), or add to chilled wines in summer to stimulate the adrenalin and cause a positive mood swing. Flowers in salads and strewn on iced cakes will contribute to health and well-being—and treat the senses aesthetically, too.

FENNEL The properties of the bulb and seeds are now well noted and are employed to ease flatulence and indigestion. Italians are hugely (and wisely) fond of the bulb, adding it to salads—and it now appears it may have especially beneficial results for women, as the chemical properties are somewhat like estrogen.

MINTS Don't overdo it, but cooking with mint will naturally freshen your breath, counter mouth complaints, and calm the nerves. An ideal choice of tea to deal with insomnia, mint settles the stomach and also helps to neutralize headache caused by tiredness and nausea. It is very easy to grow in your kitchen window.

TARRAGON The best cure for hiccups I know. Beloved of cooks for its culinary versatility, this herb was originally popular because of its capacity to aid digestion and soothe pain. Tear the leaves and scatter them over chicken and fish dishes at the last minute to keep the properties of the herb in peak form.

CARAWAY A crucial ingredient for flavoring breads, the seeds have properties similar to those of fennel and dill, but are also antispasmodic and thus a good overall health tonic. Add the young shoots of caraway to salads to sweeten the breath and relieve heartburn.

THYME This wonderful little plant is nature's own antibiotic. A cold can be nipped in the bud by making a strong tea from fresh thyme or adding thyme leaves to food. Use the oil, diluted of course, to make a therapeutic rub for the treatment of muscular aches and pains and sciatica, and to bathe in to counter depression. Boiled up with marjoram, thyme lotion (a very strong tea) makes an excellent footbath to cure blisters and corns.

MARJORAM This herb has strong sedative properties, so it must be taken cautiously; however, mild teas certainly aid restfulness. It, too, has good tonic effects and can help to ease menstrual cramps. Apart from soothing inflamed throats and mouth infections, this herb was respected by my grandmother for its ability to relieve hay fever—which she did by saturating absorbent cotton in a strong solution and inhaling it. This can also be an effective treatment for headache. My own discovery concerning this herb is its powerful capacity to heal damaged feet (see thyme, above).

BASIL The plant that needs no one to argue its case as a culinary herb. Medicinally, it has many valued properties—not least that basil tea is very effective in settling bad nerves,

and it is also known to stimulate the brain to work effectively. This makes it an ideal choice for anyone facing exams or other work stress. Wine with basil leaves steeped in it is an effective tonic and—almost certainly—has some aphrodisiac effects. Soups, stews, pasta dishes, vegetable recipes, and salads will all gain immensely from the addition of a few loosely torn basil leaves: *fresh are best*.

WATERCRESS Easily absorbed into soups, sandwiches, and salads, this herb has been used since Roman times in many interesting ways. It was thought to promote appetite, regarded for its aphrodisiac qualities, and could help to lower blood sugar levels. It is also quite simply very nutritious, and is rich in vitamins and minerals—making it a good all-purpose additive to your general diet. Externally, watercress juice was applied as a tonic for abundant, healthy hair, and it was also valued for improving skin quality.

DANDELION An essential in both of my grandmothers' salads, it was also added to wines and made into coffee substitutes. A thoroughly beneficial herb, it can be added to your diet in any way—to eat or drink—and it will flush the kidneys, help with liver complaints, purify the blood, aid digestion, act as a mild laxative or tonic, improve appetite, and probably relieve symptoms of rheumatism and arthritis. The expressed sap was once a valued treatment for warts. Drinking dandelion coffee late at night may give rise to the effect called by the French *pissenlit* (piss in bed), so be careful.

NASTURTIUM Leaves, seeds, and flowers are all valued for their tonic effects. Add the leaves and flowers to sandwiches for a lovely peppery taste, similar to watercress, and discover whether they have a positive effect on your skin, hair, nails, and eyes. The seeds are a natural antibiotic which functions without disturbing the intestinal flora, so they are useful for countering food poisoning or the onset of colds and 'flu. Like watercress, nasturtium flowers, leaves, and seeds can be used to make a strong tonic which will nourish the hair follicles and may help in preventing baldness.

WILD STRAWBERRY This was long regarded as a magic plant, and scientific research is now able to confirm many of the wild strawberry's traditionally esteemed properties. Fruits, leaves, and seeds can all be used, and have diuretic and antiseptic properties. The fruits in particular are high in iron and potassium, so they are nutritious as well as palliative. They soothe chapped and sunburned skin and help to calm an over-taxed liver.

FRENCH ROSE (*Rosa gallica*) Forever associated with life and love, the *Rosa gallica* has myriad medicinal uses, and is also delicious added to ordinary foods to improve their appeal to the senses, mind, and body. Cakes, jams, ice creams, candies, wines, and salads will all gain from the addition of *R. gallica* petals (remove the white bit at the base, which has a slightly bitter taste); crushed petals—and of course the hips in fall—form the basis of a

syrup for coughs and chest complaints. A decoction made by adding plenty of rose petals to boiling water (about 1 quart) and infusing for ten minutes will produce an excellent tonic for the old and young; it is also useful for anyone who has just finished a course of antibiotics, as it re-establishes the intestinal flora. And, of course, it will always cheer the spirits to see roses added to anything.

GARLIC If you don't find this bulb unpleasant, let it form the basis of a healthy diet. A powerful antiseptic and antibiotic, it is a brilliant general tonic, promotes appetite, can be used to treat diarrhea, nausea, and stomach cramps; is good for the circulatory system (and therefore, the heart); and relieves cold and flu symptoms. Along with onions, it reduces blood pressure, aids digestion, eliminates toxins from the system, and regulates all the vital organs, including the blood sugar level. Use fresh bulbs, as prolonged storage reduces the impact of the plant. And, if the smell really offends you, try chewing copious quantities of parsley to counteract this.

PARSLEY Not to be taken by pregnant women. This herb has legendary powers to counter the strong smells of garlic and onions, freshens the breath, disguises drinking, and is said to be an aphrodisiac. It also aids digestion, eases flatulence, and, with a high vitamin C and iron content, is a good tonic and additive to salads. The expressed juice treats bruises as well as ear- and toothache.

CILANTRO (CORIANDER) A stimulant herb, coriander is prized as an aphrodisiac and believed to combat fatigue and apathy. The Chinese have regarded it as the bestower of immortality. The seeds have a mildly narcotic effect, are sedative, and ease headache, tension, and nervous exhaustion.

CHERVIL Valued since the Middle Ages for its medicinal properties, this pleasant-tasting herb is diuretic, cleanses the liver and kidneys, and was used to bathe women in after they had given birth—possibly because of its reputation for dissolving blood clots. Today it is still used as a mild but effective eyewash (boil 2 oz. of fresh leaves in a quart of water, strain, cool, and use as a compress for those suffering tired or inflamed eyes, or for the treatment of styes). Added to salads, the leaves provide extra flavor and are a good general tonic.

ROSEMARY The most famous ingredient of "Hungary water," which was considered an elixir of youth, rosemary is certainly a cardio-tonic, stimulant herb which works as an antiseptic, diuretic, and antispasmodic. A mild infusion (like a light tea) made from flowering tips and leaves is a good tonic for convalescents and anyone suffering depression or anxiety. As a stronger tonic for external bathing, the herb treats bruises, sprains, and blisters, and helps to heal wounds.
It also seems to have a stimulating effect on the brain and memory.

CALENDULA This lovely herb, whose petals look delightful in salads or soups, reduces fevers, soothes intestinal disorders, is antiseptic and antifungal, and helps to heal skin problems.
It is also used as a rinse for the hair, to lighten it. My grandmother swore by it taken for a week before menstruation, to ease the pain and PMT (as we would now say) and to regularize the cycle altogether. It is also valuable as an external wash for eczema, burns, and bruises.

LAVENDER The medicinal properties long ascribed to lavender have now been backed up by modern research. This sedative, tranquilizing herb has been used for centuries to counter insomnia, headache, nervous stress, fever, flu, and other respiratory disorders, and externally—as a compress or bath—to treat burns and bacterial skin problems. Nowadays the oil replaces the need for making strong decoctions, and just a drop used neat on a burn or bite will speed healing and ease the pain. The flavor is also inspirational in cakes, jellies, ice creams, and fish or meat dishes. It may assist in the prevention of hair loss, eases rheumatic complaints, and helps cell renewal. A must for the senses as well as the first aid kit.

HOPS have long been valued for their aromatic, preserving qualities, as well as their general tonic effect. In a nonalcoholic form (an infusion can be made from crumbled cones), hops are sedative and calming, aid the digestive process, counter irritation and insomnia, and soothe headache. The young shoots may be eaten, like asparagus.

MEADOWSWEET The favorite herb of Queen Elizabeth 1, this plant was held sacred by the Druids, as it made the heart glad and was a general analgesic; indeed, it does contain salicylic acid and thus eases pain in much the way that aspirin does. Steeped in beer and wine, it makes a delicious, heady brew; and as a weak tea it may help with the elimination of cellulitis. Its delicious perfume made it a favorite strewing herb in Elizabethan times.

LEMON BALM (*Melissa*) Paracelsus deemed it the reviver of the spirits, and this wonderful herb is another essential in the witches' pantry. The sedative properties make it a good ingredient in herb pillows, but the antispasmodic properties also render it a good de-stressing herb ideal for women who are tense and premenstrual. In fact, lemon balm is highly regarded as a gentle aphrodisiac as it calms the nerves and lifts the spirits. The leaves are wonderful added to sandwiches and salads, omelettes, or fish dishes; it also adds a tangy lemon flavor to candies and cakes. It is an ideal general tonic and is easily grown, even throughout winter. Make a tea (infusing 1 oz. of fresh leaves in 2 cups boiled water for five minutes); sweetened with honey, it could promote longevity.

EVENING PRIMROSE A herb now much in vogue, evening primrose has been used since the seventeenth century in Europe in a syrup form to counter asthma and heavy, chesty coughs. It also has gastrointestinal uses, and is now valued for its gammalinoleic acid, which the body uses to produce prostaglandins. This helps to maintain and replenish healthy tissue and promote a sense of well-being. The expressed oil (most easily bought in capsule form) may help in the prevention of heart problems and menstrual tension, as well as improving skin and nail condition. Much has been said about its capacity to balance too much alcohol consumption—taken in a decent quantity just before bed, it may indeed reduce the effects of a hangover.

VIOLET Granny's best saved for last. This sweetly fragrant, fragile-looking flower was beloved of the Greeks and Romans, and also by the Emperor Napoleon. It conferred fertility, was requisite in love potions, and made a delicious, fragrant wine. Valued for treating headache, migraine, insomnia, and nervous tension, it contains the glycoside of salicylic acid (aspirin again), and the leaves and flowers are mildly laxative. Tea, or a stronger syrup, brewed from the leaves will aid the treatment of coughs and colds, which is why it is sometimes available as a throat pastille. Violets were popularly believed to help cure cancer, but more tests need to be carried out to qualify this claim. Use the flowers—leaves too—in cakes and salads and enjoy the aroma they release as you dine.

USING HERBS

Every day, fill a large salad bowl with as many herby leaves and flowers from this list as you can manage. Spread the good practice by inviting a friend over for lunch to talk through and ease problems. The release of difficulties is vital to daily well-being, for problems hung on to are ultimately the cause of many serious health problems.

Make compresses, and muslin herb bags for use in the bath, when the spirits are under attack, drawing information and inspiration from the plants listed. Choose an appropriate moment to boost your psychological and physical self-healing before things get out of hand.

THE RAINBOW OF SCENT. A different, soothing oil should be placed in every room and in the office: this is the "rainbow of scent". The scents listed include a balance of low, middle, and high notes (speaking "perfumely"), and help to balance your mood and sensitivity. If you are too sensitive, little things inflame your emotions. If you are insensitive, you cannot respond warmly to the needs of those closest to you. BALANCE IS ALL.

Some scents can be blended for perfect harmony. To counter general anxiety—the root of most poor health—blend ten drops each of Roman chamomile, lavender, and sandalwood in 1 fl. oz. of base oil for bathing and massage, or disperse in equal amounts in a burner.

For nervous exhaustion—especially if it is emotionally inspired—balance ten drops each of rose attar, geranium, and sandalwood, and use as above. Massage is the best method of dealing with this problem—so you need a friend to minister to you, or vice versa. If you feel yourself reaching a serious state of tension, seek professional counseling; but it will also help to burn a predominantly rose attar/lavender scent combination in your work and home area. A few days off, with plenty of restful sounds and scents, may be enough to bring the situation back under control: but strike as soon as you feel under stress.

Lavender, frankincense, and marjoram in equal amounts, and dealt with as above, will help you to counter a growing sense of panic. Peppermint and grapefruit will help you deal with fatigue and mental apathy—blend with lavender or marjoram if you simply feel mentally debilitated.

The basis of personal beauty—and projecting the best you have—is to feel a sense of your own self-worth. Contentment and joy radiate from within, showing on the outside. So, to look your best on the outside, work on the inside. Including the herbs listed on pages 138–40 in your diet will help hugely—giving you energy, good skin, and radiant health. The rainbow of scent will contribute to beauty, too. Hyacinth, rose, and sandalwood will improve your feelings about yourself—the start of looking good. Jasmine, patchouli, and orris make us joyful—and this helps us to radiate beauty to others. Make these blends part of your daily routine. Equal amounts can be blended together to produce a wonderful fragrance, which can be misted into the air by way of a plant spray bottle; add the oils to clear spring water and mist it into the room where you are working, or onto fabric to carry for a little longer. Spray some on your hair after shampooing and conditioning—for scent remains longest on your hair.

MUSIC

Music is also important to health and resilience. Sounds heal us. Musical notes are a vibratory force which combine to emit a color all their own, and these colors speak directly to our souls and hearts. Always work with music that lifts you; and when working magic surround yourself with music that has a soothing, uplifting, vitalizing, emotionally charged impact to suit the subject matter of whatever you are working on.

MASTER SPELL: **FOR GOOD HEALTH.** This spell uses a small marble statue with ivy bound around the brow (you could use an existing one from your garden, or another outside statue, just as easily as a small portable bust-size one); you will design a pentagram five-pointed (star) from forest-green ribbon, and a single candle will burn next to it, also in deep forest-green.

There are no variations: this one spell can be used for any health problem, and for any person. Use it to drive away the first signs of bad health, or to work a spell for generally atttacting good health, or for working a vigil while someone else is ill.

YOU WILL NEED
Ivy; a small statue (as above); 11/2 yards of deep forest-green ribbon; a small piece of handmade paper, scented with the oil (as below); pine, sandalwood, cedarwood, or rosewood oil; a deep forest-green pillar candle.

MOON PHASE: *Waning, if you are driving away bad health; waxing, if you are trying to attract lasting good health.*

Start by choosing your music: a Gregorian chant, or other ecclesiastical music, is very soothing and creates serenity, but use whatever makes you feel comfortable. Secure the ivy around the brow of the statue with a small bow cut from the green ribbon, and sing a song of enchantment and serenity as you bind it. Then write your name, or that of the ill person you are helping, on a slip of handmade paper, which you have first impregnated with one of the oils above—or you can select your own favorite from the "rainbow of scent." It is important to choose a scent you like, for it is to represent your—or your friend's or relative's—healthy, happy, resilient spirit. Scent the paper by placing it in

a drawer or box containing scented absorbent cotton and leave it overnight. Handmade paper is usually very porous and will take on the scent easily. Tuck the paper underneath the statue.

Now make up a five-pointed star from the green ribbon: each side should be about 10–12 in. long. Place the pillar candle to one side of the star—or if you prefer, put it in the center. Touch the ivy and the statue, caressing the head, and then light the candle: whisper a prayer-wish for, as Keats said, *"Sweet dreams, and health, and quiet breathing."* "Breathe in" the green from the ribbon and the candle; take it right into your system, and imagine green vitality, resilience, longevity. See yourself or the person you are helping like a tree in spring, sprouting blossoms of new life after the low ebb of winter.

Be thoroughly peaceful, and let the candle burn for about an hour. Concentrate from time to time on the brow of the statue and your name underneath, seeing strength entering the pores of your body and the depth of your soul. Think a little of anyone else who needs bolstering in this way, and envision them growing stronger too. Breathe in the fragrance from the oil on the paper—if you slip it out to inhale the scent, slip it back again.

Repeat this procedure two or three times more over the next few days, then treasure up the ivy and tie it around the slip of paper like a scroll. Seal it finally with a few drops of the green wax, then put it somewhere safe.

THE

REED MOON COINCIDES IN THE NORTHERN

HEMISPHERE WITH THAT PERIOD OF EARLY NOVEMBER WHEN

THE WINTER IS COMING ON SWIFTLY AND WE THINK OF THE HEARTH—

LIGHTING THE FIRES—AT HOME. THIS ALSO IS THE MOMENT WHEN LARGE

BONFIRES ARE LIT OUTSIDE, RECALLING HALLOWEEN AND, IN ENGLAND, GUY FAWKES

NIGHT, WHICH BOTH FALL WITHIN THIS MONTH. AT THIS TIME, TRY TO HAVE A FIRE LIT IN

SOME WAY WITHIN YOUR DOMESTIC ENVIRONMENT. THIS COULD TAKE THE FORM OF A CANDLE,

BUT IT IS WONDERFUL IF YOU CAN MANAGE A SMALL OPEN FIRE. THE REED'S CLOSEST ASSOCIATION

12 : HOME AND HEARTH

WITH THE HOME WAS ITS USE AS FUEL, IN RUSH MATTING ON THE FLOOR AND, MOST IMPORTANTLY,

FOR THATCHING. IT HAS COME TO SYMBOLIZE HOME LIFE FOR THE PURPOSES OF MAGIC—

AND MOST ESPECIALLY, IT IS THE MOON AND "TREE" MOST CONCERNED WITH PROTECTION.

THUS, ANY SPELL FOR BLESSINGS ON YOUR HOME—OR MAGIC WORKED TO PROTECT YOUR

HOME OR ATTRACT A NEW ONE—SHOULD BE DONE NOW. HERE WE EXPLORE WAYS

OF HONORING THE SPIRITS OF THE HOME AND DECORATING YOUR HOUSE

TO IMPROVE YOUR HEALTH, PROSPERITY AND HAPPINESS: A SORT OF

WITCHES' FENG SHUI. THE RIGHT CHOICES OF COLOR AND

DESIGN COULD ENHANCE YOUR WHOLE FUTURE

WAY OF LIVING.

Reed Moon—Moon of Home and Hearth. Color: White (overlaid with a tapestry of other colors to adjust mood and need within the home). Scents: Basil (sanctity), Jasmine (luxury), Melissa (female), Pine (male), Tuberose (joy). Number: 12. Now is the moment for recharging ourselves, and this chapter concerns the space in which to do it. This is where we focus on the love of the home.

"Piper sit thee down and write
In a book that all may read'. .
So he vanished from my sight
And I plucked a hollow reed."
from the introduction to
"Songs of Innocence"
William Blake

In the American "log-cabin pattern" quilt, the fiery red patch at the center of the block symbolized the "home fires burning"— which was then, as now, indicative of someone to come home to. All that follows is about the life force of the home itself and how to ensure a happy, blessed dwelling.

A part of your home must always remain sacred. There is an old tradition of constructing an altar, not just for the purposes of your magic-making, but also because it is thought essential to invite the world at large—and the deity therein—into your own home to create a microcosm of the blessed realm: "As above, so below." Thus you should have a designated space that is your permanent altar—a small area set aside in which nothing material or functional is to occur except your thanks, and spell-prayers, being offered up: a place of calm.

However, various aspects of your home should be altars to different ends. Your bedroom should be an altar to rest and peace, as well as to love. Your kitchen should be an altar to health and hospitality. Your bathroom should be an altar to health and purity; your office to wisdom and higher thought, as well as material success. Your "hearth" room—the heart of the home, or living room—should be an altar to the love of all beings; so let us begin here.

Creating the Altar of the Blessed House
Your home should contain one small space that enacts, physically, a prayer for blessings within your home and family existence there. It should include emblems strong enough to exude a powerful, magnetic pull on positive energy, which will be enticed to take up residence with you. This small area was customarily in the room of the fire—the living area where all the family gathered for strength; so you must designate a little table or window sill, or a space beside a fireplace if you have one, in which to lay out your pictorial message to the deity.

A Beehive is the witches' symbol for happy, harmonious home life—everyone dwelling together making a honeyed existence. Also, a Shell, which signifies an exotic home, is especially symbolic of hopes of going somewhere special and dwelling in a romantic, dream home. This is partly because shells come from water, the element of emotion. To create an altar to the deity for your strong wish of dwelling within a supportive, romantic, peaceful abode, draw upon these symbols in any combination you feel comfortable with, and create a signature altar. You might, for example, use beeswax candles, and replenish them on a regular basis; or you might find a simple honey-fragranced candle next to which you might place a small silver or jeweled bee. Some companies actually make a beehive candle; or you might find another way to represent a "honeyed home" that is personal to you. I have a beautiful African basket containing nautilus shells on my altar, to keep a prayer lit for those dear to me who live thousands of miles away: part of my home is in the English countryside, and part in sunny Sydney by the water, where my mother and sister and some friends live. The shells, alongside my candles, link me to both homes.

If you feel your home has been under siege from negative or unhappy people who perhaps have visited or stayed, walk through each day with some incense to cleanse the area, and leave it burning on your altar next to the candles, shells, or whatever you have chosen. It is good to do this even if you know you yourself have been stressed more than usual; OUR HOMES ARE OUR SHELLS AND SOMETIMES THEY NEED STRENGTHENING.

OTHER ALTARS

It is valid to create support altars in separate spaces. A bedroom should contain an "ALTAR TO LOVE," incorporating colors and emblems from chapter 3. Place a shell there too, if your partner is a foreigner, or loves the sea—or if you do. Place a growing plant there if you want to show that your love continues to grow and learn. The kitchen will have, perhaps, A HERBAL ALTAR, where potted herbs or related plants are grown, which can become the focus of some kitchen candles, and colors, ribbons and/or emblems drawn from chapter 11, on health. If you are preparing a feast for a special occasion, incorporate some additional material in your "kitchen altar" from the celebratory suggestions in chapter 10.

Near your front door or in your entrance hall, your altar will be simple but could contain, besides the candle, an acorn or oak leaf. Your reference points will be drawn from chapter 7, covering security and strength. Perhaps burn some frankincense or sandalwood incense near your door to welcome people and attune them to your positivity. In other words, you are asking your guests' subconscious minds to leave their doubts and angers at the door as they come in.

Your study, office, or desk area will be dedicated to either wisdom and knowledge (chapter 9) or work (chapter 4), or both. If you are an artist, you might draw on some ideas from chapter 2, on vision. If you are an excellent starter of projects but not always a finisher, try adding in some colors and thoughts from the final chapter, on completion, to ensure that you get to the end of your work. Again, decide on the combination of pictograms and symbols, colors and scents that appeal to you from the suggestions given, and make them personal to you in some way, so that you can read the ideas you have woven into your environment and be reminded of their function for you.

To sum up, the idea of constructing the altars is, if you like, based on similarities. Your altar is a microcosm of sympathetic elements drawn together, peacefully and aesthetically, to enact a strong psychological message of harmony, strength, joy, and so on. Your thoughts make the connection between the existing miniature "theater" of your altar and your own home and life. It is that simple—and highly effective. Your wishes are the key: wish strongly, and you will have an impact on the real world around you.

DECORATING YOUR HOUSE: **A WICCAN FENG SHUI.** The elements of fire, earth, air, and water are vital to the components of magic and worship: we are grateful for all of them in our lives, and honor them in magic. All must be placed somewhere in your home to draw into it the requisite elements of a good, balanced life.

Although the most obvious principal element of this chapter is fire, water is also significant, because it was believed that fire and water were the two most important elements of creation. Thus, in "feng shui for witches," these two elements must be in balance everywhere.

THE BEDROOM

This should contain all the elements, to rebalance the renewing soul during rest. Hence the advice regarding the altar, where a plant growing in a pot, basket, or windowbox will symbolize life on earth and place the all-important symbolic element of our planetary home close to our resting souls. Always have a growing plant in your bedroom, as well as on your main "HEARTH" altar. Choose a cyclamen, traditionally, if you want the plant to do the job of adding protection to your home, plus roses, pansies, peonies, or any combination of the three, for pure love.

Flowers in glass (which has come through fire) filled with water, and flowers placed in a metal vase (for metal comes through both fire and earth) will combine the elements of emotion (water), passion (fire), and good sense (metal/earth). A window opened for at least half an hour every day, even in winter, admitting air, will make the vital link with this element. Air also symbolizes the medium of our carried thoughts and prayers, so it is essential to open a window for a moment in the morning, to invite your dreams into the real world outside.

A mirror is vital for bouncing thoughts from: bad ones away from you, good ones toward you. There should always be two mirrors in the bedroom (as well as two in the bathroom, a large one near the front door, and two in your main living area —though one of them might not necessarily be seen— see below), and it is lucky to place colored pouches behind them. Have a pink pouch filled with roses and lavender for reflecting romantic and passionate love, and another of your own choice of color and content, depending on what you feel is most lacking in your life. It might be material strength, luck, knowledge, protection. Go back to the appropriate chapter and decide what is required most for you. Placing the representative herb/flower, color, and scent in a pouch tied behind the mirror will place that dream into your dream world, and bring it closer to reality.

Candles must abound in the bedroom, as everywhere. Choose colors for love and sex in your bedroom, scent them, and play massage games by candlelight. This not only is romantic (disguising our imperfections by softer light) but also carries the element of passion as we touch each other. If you have a fireplace in your bedroom, put a candle near this; if not, find a safe, appropriate home for this all-important medium of love.

In the past, herbs were always strewn in the house and especially in the bedroom. This was mainly to counteract the really unsanitary smells and conditions we would now find intolerable, but it is still magical to step on herbs and release their odor as well as their properties. If you live in a warm climate and don't have a carpeted floor, you could strew a few fresh herbs on the floor to create a cloud of heady possibilities in your bedroom—as indeed in any room (the bathroom and living area respond well to this). Traditional choices are lady's bedstraw, sweet woodruff, violet, lavender, peony, and clary. Inevitably, it is difficult to find these herbs fresh throughout the year unless you grow them, but it is well worthwhile making your own herb pillow from fresh plants you have ordered from a specialist supplier. Add in the flowers of various tranquilizing herbs to give you a restful night's sleep: lavender is relaxing, but also intoxicates the sensual zones; lilac is very soothing and also drowses tensions away; evening primrose will counteract inebriation—so is terrific if you've had a few too many. If you have overeaten, try chamomile and fennel in a pillow, as an herb tea in a special bedtime set, or crushed under your feet before bed; jasmine and honeysuckle flowers are a straight choice for sexual enticement. Every couple of weeks you could cram a selection of these herbs, chosen for their individual properties, into a muslin bag tied with ribbon.

For lovemaking, specifically, nothing will improve upon scented candles floating hedonistically in beautiful glass bowls. The best fragrances are, again, honeysuckle, bluebell or hyacinth, jasmine, and vanilla. Floating them—with a few small fresh flowers—in reflective glass bowls filled with water will introduce the elements of fire, earth, and water, create beautiful light illusions, and an air redolent of exquisite sensuality. This can also be achieved through mixing your own essential oil combination, put into a base of pure spring water, which is then spritzed onto your pillows. I have a small plant spray bottle into which I put clear spring water and add fresh oils each week: vetiver, lemongrass, and sandalwood for sleep, lavender and geranium, rose attar and tuberose for more active evenings. Benefits are mutual: you will thank yourself, and be thanked. Moreover, you have taken the trouble to achieve something out of the ordinary, especially if you vary your scents and color combinations regularly.

And finally, ribbons and music. Tie the former into clouds above you, as representative wishes for what you want. Create a soft canopy of muslin or other cotton fabric above your head to send your thoughts soaring into the clouds, and tie the corners with blue ribbons for eternal love, red for passion at the beginning of a love affair, pink for perpetual love, yellow for intellect, green for healing, and each and every color you have learned about throughout this book.

Music is the language of the gods: the very word "enchantment" carries the song of ecstasy—the music of the spheres. Hearing is a primary sense: we need to listen to the sounds of beauty in the world to recreate beauty in our lives. So, arrange music in your sleeping environment, to soothe, to excite, to calm, to ignite. It is far more important than a television set to a magic life. It will feed and support your mind, calm your overstretched senses, create mood for sexual pleasure, and even lift you into realms of the godlike, uncovering the possibility of genuinely divine intimacy in accord with the Mozartian proposition.

THE HEARTH ROOM (OR LIVING ROOM)

Look for the "soul" of the space you principally live in—especially near a fireplace, or a special feature that you feel magnetically drawn to. Adorn this area, and give it a special "battery." You may do this by laying out fresh flowers and potted plants or placing candles; but the most important thing is that you must create a "hearth" (literally, the heart of the home), even if it is only a painting of a fire glowing. At the very least, cluster candles of many shapes and sizes together—perhaps in glass jars or divided boxes—and make a space around them. Place a small mirror somewhere near your candlelit hearth to reflect the light and positivity you create here. It need only be small, but find a mirror that fits the mood of your little area, and make sure that the candlelight bounces off it to illuminate the parallel world.

Once you have your "hearth," release aromatics into the air to attract the divine and neutralize pain and anxiety. In many cultures this was done very simply: pinecones and resins formed the centre of many a log fire, as did other perfumed woods like cedar and rosewood. To clear the head and attract positive spirits, beautiful herbs and spices were burned on incense burners such as charcoal burners. It is now easy to find these commercially and to buy incense mixture in jars instead of the usual sticks; or, you can make up your own blend of precious spices to burn in this same way. Alternatively, place some vaporizing oils next to your hearth.

Traditional scents for the purification and harmonizing of the heart of the home are pine resin and oil and bergamot (for the male element, and thus very important if there is a lack of male energy in your house); melissa, cinnamon, and vanilla (for the female element); rosemary and basil, which can be burned dried or fresh in a fireplace to clear the mind and invite focused thought into your home; benzoin, frankincense and myrrh, for the deity; and rose and tuberose, for love in the home.

Scent candles with these oils, as a way of dispersing these aromas into the heart and life-pulse of your home. Even carry this benediction into temporary homes: take an appropriately fragranced candle into a vacation house or hotel room, and make gifts of these to friends with whom you are going to stay.

Plants must grow somewhere in your central room, and they must look healthy. These symbolically oxygenate your world, and to do this they should exude color as well as fresh air. Choose plants with blue flowers, plus red or pink, and white or golden yellow. Others may be seasonal options, but these are the requirements for stability, loyalty, insight, and love. If you want to dedicate one plant to the divine, choose something regal and white, and tie the pot or bucket it is planted in with a white ribbon. My own choice would be a lily (also for the perfume), some jasmine, or an orchid. This invites the highest, noblest spirit into your home.

The scents and plants see to our senses of smell and sight. Touch, hearing, and taste must also be satisfied in our key room. Tactile fabrics and floor surfaces are essential in this one place. As a follower of Wicca thinking and an adept exponent of the craft of magic thought and spell-making, you must pay attention to enhancing all your senses all the time. Thus, bring your feeling capacity into total consciousness in this room, and your other senses will also engage more fully.

Velvet pillows and throws are invaluable in your living room. They bid you to relax, unwind, loosen up, feel good in your own body; they slow you down and turn off anxiety; they welcome others with their message of comfort and luxury. Choose a rainbow of colors and make them appear and disappear as required: olive green and mulberry, remember, will encourage you to be wise, so place these in an "adult chair," or use them on top of other colors when you feel a call to be especially together mentally. Go to reds if you are initiating something in your lounge area, and pinks and lavenders for love. Tactile rugs have the same function: they, too, can be changed around seasonally according to your color needs—but always lift your physical senses with fabric furnishings that, literally, turn you on.

Remember that tiled and ceramic surfaces signal your senses to a different kind of touch: an interplay of stone and brick, tile and wood will keep you alert and ensure that your senses are constantly alive. This is all the more true if you pad

through your home in very soft shoes, or bare feet. Sound is—for me, clairaudient since childhood—the most important sense to satisfy in this central room of the happy home. I can live without trips abroad, but never without good sound equipment and a wonderfully varied collection of music to soothe my nerves and encourage my soul to yearn for something better.

Chanting, as I have said, is the key to magic at the highest level; it enters your being on the vibratory airwaves, and is the channel to the soul. Words spoken have a magic property; sound travels through time. Chanting also induces a meditative state by virtue of its repetition, and is fundamental to all prayer; but you do not have to play Gregorian chant to induce your own level of religious being. Play any music that makes your soul happy: then send transcendental thought through the ether.

Sound should surround you—so organize your equipment, insofar as possible, to achieve this, with speakers in balanced corners of your hearth room. Never allow negative or ugly sound into your hearth room for long; these vibratory waves have a lingering effect of melancholy, so balance your amount of Mahler, or songs of heartbreak, or heavy metal, with sounds of pure harmonious glory. When spell-making, try the exercise of sending thoughts to another soul while listening to music you know you both like. The music waves should deepen your focus and recall of the other person.

Taste ought to be catered for in any way possible—but unobtrusively in this area. The throne of taste is the kitchen, but here, by the hearth, have a small bowl of nuts, olives, or candies to entice the taste buds and offer something in this department. A large bowl of colorfully wrapped chocolates will almost always have your visitors (and you) salivating. Quality is the essence—not quantity. A yoga teacher I know in Sydney always has a handful of smoked almonds in his living room with which to welcome his guests; and nuts are traditionally a

blessing from the gods.

And finally, the sixth sense. How could we leave out this unquantified element? Your main living area might show some reference (as veiled as you like) to the spiritual realm and the gift of extra sight and power you wish to find within. Discreetly, put a pentagram—A FIVE-POINTED STAR—in your hearth room. It could simply take the form of a leftover Christmas star if you want to be mysterious, but it is lovely to tape out a little pentagram in colored ribbon: white, yellow, red, blue, purple. Make it tiny, but utter all of your general prayers over the pentagram and light a candle in the center.

Ribbons, glassware, crystals, bells and chimes, and symbolic items can be chosen entirely from your own guidance on the subject: this is your home, and should meet your needs and taste. Take inspiration, perhaps, from the ideas in some of the earlier chapters, but always be guided by your own ultimate inclination—for it will be right for you.

A MAGIC KITCHEN

This does not begin with a shopping list for cauldrons or a witches' broom, though have these if you like. Kitchens begin with the host's feeling of hospitality and magic radiated to the world. The food you prepare here will have the power to change people who eat with you—so integrity and good hygiene are the key points.

Always have at least one growing herb to symbolize growing health in the area of nourishment. A potted supermarket plant, replaced weekly, is better than nothing; and a windowbox of seeds lovingly planted by you, herbs growing cheek by jowl with flowering ornamentals, is the best kitchen positivity I can think of. Again, have a tiny mirror above your cooking place to send packing gremlins who would spoil your food—never bake a cake without this failsafe.

A well-lit kitchen is also much desired by the witchy cook, and is sometimes a problem for those dwelling in a small space where a kitchen has been carved out of no space at all.

Try to ameliorate this with good lighting: light and sunshine are the first ingredients of positivity that you want to incorporate into your cooking, to create sunshiny characters at your table. Is this why such extraordinary hospitality is inherent in the people of Mediterranean lands?

Remember candles in the kitchen: light and prayer are as important here as anywhere else in the house.

THE STUDY

An important area for many, as it is the place of serious thought and perhaps material stability, the study/office deserves a short entry of its own.

Tie many things in clusters with ribbons. Books tied with ribbons will celebrate knowledge and symbolize what there is still to learn. A dish of water, in a wood or metal bowl, should be near your working and living spaces. This also adds moisture back into the rooms when winter heat takes it from the air.

Counteract the impersonal effect of electronic equipment: if you have PCs, fax machines, printers, and other computerized elements in your work space, offset this with plants, goldfish, or photographs of people you love, in order to introduce a human element. Go to work on herb pillows and ribbons to introduce feeling and scent into what might otherwise be a sterile atmosphere. Grow one luxury plant, with a coin pushed into the soil, for certainty of perpetuating your work and cash in the future. An orchid, jade plant, or any small fruiting tree will be symbolic of the fruits of labor and fertility.

AND GENERALLY . . .

These are thoughts to consider when energizing your whole house to a positive existence.

- MIRRORS can be placed in the hall or near the front door (to reflect back the quality of thought sent to you, to re-bless those who send you love and fend off those who send you thorns), and in the bathroom, not only for practical reasons but also to aid you in your quest for personal health and beauty. A bathroom mirror should be an object of beauty itself, and should be carefully chosen to reflect you at your best. Cheap mirrors will fail to do this, and may send you off into the world grumpy, dejected, and lacking confidence.

- CANDLES should abound—everywhere. They are your link with past, present, and future, your thoughts sent into the atmosphere, and your hopes borne aloft. Buy the best you can afford, and replace them as they are used up. Ask for candles as presents from friends: a candle given has special value.

- SCENT your home with lavender and other healing/balancing scents. Every room should have a scented oil burner, which can disseminate a different mood-scent in each place.

- Make something at the fire on a regular basis: toasting bread is an age-old symbol of the daily grain renewed by fire— and it is delicious. The same can be done with chestnuts, marshmallows, or even pinecones and other woods for scent.

)

MASTER SPELL: **TO BLESS YOUR DWELLING.** This spell is based around a white seashell; it uses a beautiful key from one of the locks in your door, next to the seashell, and the magic must be worked at some kind of fireplace. (There are no candles in this spell—just a fire.)

YOU WILL NEED

5 white ribbons, each 12 in. long; a fireplace (an open fire, such as a barbecue, will do if there really is nothing better); a perfect white conch or nautilus seashell; a key from the prettiest lock in your house (if you have only one door, get a special key cut and have it silverplated for this spell); benzoin incense; a pinecone; a small piece of paper on which to write your address.

MOON PHASE: *Full.*

Deep-breathe on the full moon: draw the light right into your soul. Lay out the five lengths of ribbon into a five-pointed star, which you will place before the hearth or fireplace. In the center of the star, place the shell. Now take your key, offer it for blessing to the moon, and make a prayer over it that the inhabitants of the house, and the events that occur within it, will be blessed with luck and light, goodness and wisdom. Ask, too, for wisdom within your own domain: in other words, that decisions you make within your home will be the right ones. Lay the key beside the shell, and wish for a happy, romantic home.

Light the fire and burn some of the benzoin incense and pinecones in it; waft the scents through the space you are working in, and across the nearby shell and key.

Finally, write your address on a small piece of paper, purify it in the scented smoke, and ask particularly for protection from fire and tempest. Wish hard for several moments for a truly sound domestic life—for simple blessings on your home; then burn the paper completely in the fire.

The spell is complete as the fire burns low; but keep the shell and key for an altar in your home, and light a candle by them regularly.

THE ONLY VARIATION IS FOR A NEW HOME.

Before you move into a new dwelling, put ribbon (forest-green, or cherry-pink if it is a house you are moving into with a lover—or both together) across the door, and cut it, both of you together, with new scissors. Then perform the spell as above, placing the new scissors in conjunction with the shell and the key. Keep the ribbon tied near the door ever after.

It

is time for us to say "thank you" and

to give back to the spirit of the world. We now arrive

full circle at thirteen—the witches' number—corresponding

to the elder moon, the moon of completion, covering the period from

late November to late December. This brings us to a chapter of many

blessings—the finishing touch to all magic, for fullest power. Much of this

magic concerns saying "thank you" when magic-making has produced good effect.

Once your wish has been granted, it is good manners to thank the powers

13 : COMPLETION

that be for turning your mental strength

into material manifestation. The "blessings" might include the extras in life, such as

money superfluous to real requirements, or an extra child, or some other additional

bounty. The magic-making includes advice for "letting go"—either of a marriage

partner at the time of a divorce to keep it amicable, or of a relative or friend

who "goes away," perhaps even to die. All things have their time and place,

and this kind of magic is as important as any other. We learn to

recognize the cycle of death and rebirth: after this, the

individual has completed all life's lessons, and

should practice them for the benefit

of all.

ELDER MOON—MOON OF COMPLETION AND WHOLENESS. Color: GOLD. Scents: ORANGE, NEROLI, BERGAMOT, CITRUS, ROSE, PINE. Number: 13.

This last moon in the year, which falls across the period of Yule, is governed by the beautiful wintry elder moon, which rules magic of completeness, wholeness, new cycles, and rebirth.

"Weave a circle round him thrice,
 And close your eyes with holy dread,
 For he on honey-dew hath fed,
 And drunk the milk of Paradise."
"KUBLA KHAN"
SAMUEL TAYLOR COLERIDGE

The hollow stem of elder, with the pith scooped out, was used to rekindle fires and make them burn hotter—literally, to give life to a dying fire—and it has always been closely associated with witchcraft and magic. It was believed that a dryad, or tree nymph, dwelled within the heart or branches of the tree, so this was not a tree from which to make furniture or to burn carelessly on a fire. This tradition persists among country people today, who may regard the tree as bad luck; its spirit would haunt anyone who abused its soul!

The elder tree is one of the most useful for ailments contracted at this chilly time of year—which is why it was so valuable to witches. Elder has been revered for its medicinal properties forever, and seemingly by all peoples. It appears in the Jewish Kabbala, and was allegedly the tree by which Judas hanged himself (for it is a tree of justice, which demands great respect); in some traditions Christ's cross on Calvary was made from it. Certainly, country people may still be observed doffing their caps to the Elder Mother to beg her good grace, and her protective powers are sought in the afterlife: branches were once buried with the dead to protect them from evil spirits on their last journey! Thus, too, the elder tree and moon make the finaljourney in the dying year, to ensure rebirth (the close connection here with the Christmas "birth" celebration is clear).

In the past all parts of the tree were used in healing, but as we are now aware of the toxic properties of the leaves and berries, only the beautiful, sweet-fragranced flowers are generally used and other parts of the plant should be avoided, although the berries are boiled to make syrups which are powerful remedies against respiratory congestion and coughs. Raw berries and the leaves should never be taken.

The healing elder flowers, which can be cooked up in a variety of ways, help hay fever and asthma sufferers and are a good source of vitamin C, which explains their long history of use as a treatment for colds and to reduce fevers; they make a delicious wine or champagne and can be harvested in high summer, then bottled and left to mature. This makes them the perfect toast for a "thank you" for good fortune in the year, under the elder moon, at Yuletide. If you have no access to the flowers—or no time—just add some commercially made elderflower syrup to your own champagne or white wine.

CELEBRATING YULETIDE

The feast for the elder moon is the major celebration of the year: YULE: THE FESTIVAL OF GOD—or the sun, being reborn after its symbolic death on the shortest day of the year. It has parallels across, seemingly, every civilization, and most of the present Christmas traditions can be traced to much older ceremonies, including the star of hope, the sacred candle flames, the decoration of the dwelling with evergreens, Christmas wine or "wassail," the feast, and even gift giving.

THE WREATH: To celebrate the old way, make a wreath—the symbol of the year turning full cycle, and of no beginning, no end—for the door, with a twig or leaf from every tree, and interlaced with beautiful bright flowers of many colors. The wreath is an expression of faith in the eternity of being; it is also a good symbol of openness and peace, which is complicit with the elder moon. The best wreaths will be made by you, and can in fact be of any material you like. Straw and burlap were sometimes used, as they are sacred to the crops.

THE YULE LOG: The real thing was hewn from oak, brought into the hearth with great ceremony, lit from the old fire, and tended to make sure it would not go out for at least the solstice day (December 21). It could be re-lit at sundown each day until the New Year was safely brought in—the whole object being to ensure that the sun would grow again and bring life and warmth. The Yule log was a sacred object, imbued with great magic power, and it was hoped that, from the theory that like begets like, the fire of the sun would surely return. Ashes from the log were plowed into the fields after the critical "birth" period was over.

Your log could be blessed with your own promise to generate something, according to your gift, that makes the world around you even the tiniest bit better: a witch's pledge. Sprinkle it with your favorite oils or wood shavings for scent, before you set light to it.

THE YULE CANDLES: This was another echo of the sacred flame. It was important to light the candles each night from midwinter to New Year, and the proud flame would ensure abundance in all things. Many items might be laid around the altar of the candle—from money, to food, to wassail. The remnants of the candle were married to the log and burned a last time before the ashes were sown into the soil for fertility. The whole ritual was very phallic and symbolic!

THE YULE FEAST: This, too, echoes the concept that like begets like: if there was a surfeit of food at Yule, the year would ensure plenty to eat! Of course, it was also a pleasure to create a feast to brighten the darkest day of the year, with celebration and light and joy. It was a feast to celebrate the birth of the new growing sun—the most important birthday of the year.

The principal Pagan dish—around which all other feast dishes revolved—was usually a pig, deer, or boar. The boar had an apple in its mouth to genuflect to the goddess (for whom apples were sacred), and the deer was likewise connected with the Green Man and the Holly King, as well as being sacred to the Celtic gods. The famous marriage of venison with juniper berries formed a kind of honorable offering to the cooked animal's spirit, and to the gods. Juniper was another important winter herb, for the berries were a huge help against the rheumatic and arthritic illnesses that plagued those who lived in damp, cold, northern winters.

If you wish to attain a little Pagan authenticity in your Yule feast, make or buy a chocolate yule log to finish your meal, and make a wish on it as it is cut. If you cannot quite manage a deer or a boar for your Christmas meal, try at least to incorporate apples into your more traditional fare. Decorating the table with apples sprayed gold and with mistletoe will recall the offerings to the gods to ensure a fertile and prosperous year ahead. These are decidedly Pagan symbols, as are holly and the pine tree—all of which are evergreens sacred to the magic that enticed the sun to make the earth green and fecund in this, the now waxing year.

Furthermore, nuts are often part of the Christmas table because of the Celtic practice of divining with them for what the year ahead portended: asking a question and tossing a nut into the fire would give you a "yes" or "no" answer, depending on whether the nut popped (yes) or remained dormant (no). You might try this yourself with an awareness of the origins of the custom!

CHRISTMAS PUNCH: A form of the old "WASSAIL," this was a welcome to those in the chilly night, full of spices for health and fertility in the year ahead. The name itself seems to derive from the Anglo-Saxon *wes hal,* which means "be whole"; this was the drink offered to someone's good health, and was shared communally by taking the large wassail bowl from door to door. The leftover was given as an offering to the fruit trees and the fields—a highly magical practice. Make your own from wine, to which you add spices, and invite your friends and family to a merry partaking for their health and luck, and your continued combined strength as friends and kin.

GIVING GIFTS: The tradition of presents at this peak moment of the year derives from the belief that, as like begets like, giving generously to others would ensure their goodwill, and appease the gods and implore them to favor each person with a generous bounty in the coming year. This aspect of appeasement can also be seen in the offering to St. Nicholas—whereby one would

be rewarded generously for one's own generosity!

Charms placed in the English Christmas pudding also have this aspect of offering, and of ensuring luck in the dawning year.

THE TREE: Besides being associated with Christmas, the Christmas tree embodies the godly spirit of vegetation and fecundity. During the Roman Saturnalia, pines were brought into the temples by tree-bearers, as the pine was sacred to the goddess; subsequent customs often used a bough from fruit trees instead of pine to decorate the house at Yule, ensuring a fertile year ahead. Placing certain fruit tree branches in water would encourage them to blossom—which was a good sign for the future.

The holly and ivy, which we have talked about in earlier chapters, also found a sacred place at this time of year in the home; the holly was the symbol of the waning year, and at this time the Holly King still has command, until December 21/22, when he joins in battle with the Oak King, who will govern the new growing year. Ivy is a plant of survival and resurrection right through the winter and symbolizes the movement from winter stillness and death to rebirth.

Incorporate all the customs you are familiar with and place them in their magical, Pagan context. This will joyously complete the ritual of a magical year.

THE COLOR GOLD

A color associated with the Christmas season for so long, gold is also the color of total attainment and completion. It is associated with the sun at its zenith, and here is a request to entice the sun back to its high power once more. It has connotations of joy and brilliance, associations with fire, and instills pleasure and vibrancy.

In all magic of this time, and connected with completion and seeing things through to the end, only a speck of gold is needed. It is a finishing touch: too much is gaudy, and somewhat greedy. To make the Yuletide altar, and the altar of thanks—or for urging all magic-making of the year to its final conclusion— just the smallest grain of gold, or a few grains of golden sand, or a tiny piece of golden jewelry placed by a gold candle, will be sufficient to raise a golden spirit of celebration. At any time of the year, gold should be placed next to your altar as a prayer of thanks for your spell-working being answered.

Completed work also includes helping out a friend with the working of their magic—but without improper interference. You can burn a simple, small golden candle with their name written underneath to boost their magic-working, as a kind of "shadow" of their energy. Do not be tempted to do the whole spell for them: anyone else's magic is their own karma, not yours!

The other important thing to do under this moon, and utilizing the vibrancy of gold, is to "give gold"—even the smallest amount. During this cycle, some gold must leave your hands and benefit others who have less: this is a universal "thank you" for everything. It need only be as much as you can afford— quite literally a few pennies in a collection box. Each time you have to say a "*thanks*" for your magic working well, find a recipient, and give.

For a little bit of magic in everyday life at this time of year, we should employ our magic for the benefit of all on the earth. Spend time strewing flowers on others' paths! Give a tiny bunch of winter violets, or roses, or another flower of color and fragrance, to thank those dear to you just for their friendship. Give plants regularly—tied in shiny paper with a golden bow— for the gift of growth from earth is the finest you can give.

And for a little bit of "completion magic" on your most important concerns, try tying a golden ribbon around the index finger of your dominant hand (left if you are left-handed) and concentrating on the issue itself. Send mental strength to those concerned with you in the affair, and imagine the ending you have worked for being achieved. Think of a big golden ribbon being tied around the whole matter, with a satisfactory result.

THE SCENTS OF FRUITION AND COMPLETENESS

The oils and fragrances associated with a sense of completeness, and the power to carry matters through to the end, are, not surprisingly, also connected with the powers of concentration and memory, confidence and emotional strength. Pine (a very Christmassy scent!) and bergamot, neroli, and rose are the most powerful scents for completion magic and for helping us through obstacles to the winning post.

If you feel your resolve weakening, your mind wandering, or your belief tested in your wish to see something right through to the end; or if you are tired and uncertain that your efforts will ultimately bring the goal you have striven for—this is the moment to work a little everyday magic with these oils and scents.

Bathe in rose or pine oil and breathe in the positive scent. Let your spirits rise with optimism, believe once again that all is within your grasp—that you are indeed nearly there. Fix your thoughts on your desires, and relax on them. Nervous worry is the element most likely to frustrate your work: if you believe truly that you can do something, it will be. This, then, is the "eleventh hour" spell—to convince yourself again at this last moment that all will be well, that your pains have not been in vain. Put aside doubt, and push through to your victory. Tell the spirits and the elements that you are there; lather your body in rose or pine soap, caress and pamper your mind and body, believe in yourself again. Be confident in the strength of your preparation work.

If you are going for a last interview, a final business meeting, a conclusive exam to all that has gone before, a farewell to someone you want to think well of, and they of you: prepare your thoughts and embolden your behavior with orange blossom, neroli, and bergamot scents. Burn a candle scented with one of these, and put your prayer underneath the candle foot on a piece of paper; concentrate on the matter for a few moments, then blow out your flame. Sally forth in good spirits!

If you are parting from someone you have loved, and wish to remain friendly and be grown up about the split, give them a gift of orange blossom, or mock orange, or a citrus tree, and tie it in beautiful paper fixed with a golden bow. Sincerely wish them happy and well, and you both free of each other in the best ways: your relationship will die away from its old pattern, and a new form of bond will arise—not binding, but warm and imbued with fellow-feeling. This is governed by the elder moon, for it is a death and a rebirth, and shows maturity and humanitarian roundedness.

THE NUMBER 13

In the tarot, Arcanum XIII is "DEATH," sometimes called "THE REAPER"—which is more truly a symbol of the death or culmination of one set of circumstances paving the way for a brand-new cycle, a new age. It might be termed, "The king is dead; long live the king," marking a new growth from the old branch. It is a reminder that we must witness creation, destruction, and then renewal in order to move forward. It is also highly symbolic of the transformation we make as individuals when we release ourselves from material instincts and give our soul to the universal laws of re-creation, and become a more celestial being. This expresses perfectly what we should now know from all the lessons that have gone before, bringing us to a new sense of immortality and freeing us from fetters of all kinds. We should now begin to understand what it is to be complete. THIS, THEN, IS THE WITCHES' NUMBER. LUCKY (NOT UNLUCKY) "13."

THE TASKS OF THE ELDER MOON. The elder moon is certainly about maturity, about slowing your pace a little and thinking roundly and wisely about the whole picture in any given situation. This moon's lesson is one of patience —the patience to see our tasks through to the end—and of tying up loose ends and finishing what we have taken on. Therefore, this is an important time for completing what we have set ourselves, when perhaps we had lost the way, or the impetus, or just forgotten our pledges.

The first gift is, at busy Christmas time, sometimes the hardest to give: time. We are always rushing now, but we should slow down long enough to give those who need us some of our time, even though (or perhaps especially because!) this is often more costly to us than gold. In a hurried and increasingly impersonal world, make a pact to give someone a day of your time with no strings attached. Give time, especially, to your children as a surprise. They will be happier than if you gave them a material gift. Give time to your lover or partner—the more so as your lives are usually very busy. Make time, also, for yourself: put routine and everyday duty aside long enough to think mellow thoughts. Show all those you really love how valued they are—not materially, but emotionally, and with your time.

GIVE TIME TO LETTERS: we never seem to write them anymore, but one of the good things about new technology is how easy it is to keep up a friendship by e-mail. Write someone the smallest of letters—but write it down. The written word is a permanent treasure, and we usually keep those things sent by someone we love. Make this a priority.

Also, revise anything you have written by way of short stories or poetry. If you have outstanding wishes connected with books or publishing, or if you want to submit written material to an agent or magazine, do so now, and with the golden candles and citrus, pine, or rosy scents aiding you. DON'T LEAVE YOUR DREAMS IN THE DRAWER: PUT THEM IN THE MAIL AND WISH THEM WELL!

Then turn your attention to other unfinished business. COMPLETE TASKS: burn oils of orange flower, neroli, citrus, and rose while answering correspondence, complete decorating and painting jobs, do the filing, clear out closets. As this moon coincides with Yule (Christmas), have a little pre-New Year clean-out once a year and finish old jobs. Throw wasted promises into the wastebasket—and start again. Of course you can't finish everything; but it is important to finish at least one significant thing.

MASTER SPELL: OF THANKS, AND TO ENSURE COMPLETION OF AN AMBITION.

This spell is the one to take you through to the happy ending of the fairytale. You may perform it shortly after doing magic for a particular goal, to tell the entities of the spirit world that you are confident of return; you may do it if the affair seems to "drag" a little, and you want to nudge matters along a bit faster; or you can perform it when your "wish has been granted." Don't forget! It is as important as remembering to say "thank you" to someone for a lovely gift, and ensures a strong ongoing relationship. For reasons that will become self-evident, there are again no true variations. This is another "master number" spell—not an everyday concern!

YOU WILL NEED

A "love-pillow" (see below), which is more than half of this spell; 1 leaf from every tree mentioned in the 13 moons (if you really cannot manage this, do a drawing in your own hand of the identifiable shape of each one using a good source book as your guide); 13 candles of all the colors of the moons (votive or short tapers are fine); likewise, a "set" of the 13 various ribbons, each 1 yard long; a photo album with pictures of those dearest to you, and some who perhaps are not so dear (for forgiveness, which is part of completion).

MOON PHASE: *Any.*

MAKING THE "LOVE PILLOW"

This must be an item of your own making, however inept you think you are at sewing. Make it with love and strong feeling, and it will be a powerfully woven spell. Using fabric in white or gold (brocade would also be a good choice), make a pillow stuffed with herbs, at least some of which have been home grown. It should be embroidered with threads from all the colors of the chapters (echoing the ribbons and candles) and sprinkled with all the scents, but predominantly rose, jasmine, and lavender. The idea is to embroider a symbolic word or image that says "thank you" in any form you like. Play music while you work—and work by lamp- or candlelight. The most successful pattern might be a simple circle—perhaps consisting of all the first letters of the names of those who make up your world. This spell—a piece of "WEAVING"—is your magnum opus. You should place it near your head and heart at night, and drink in wisdom, pain, strength, love, thought, and the power to conclude the things you start. It is the most powerful talisman—and should be passed on to someone you love when you take leave of this time and place.

If you really cannot make your own, buy something suitable—perhaps a lavender-scented bed pillow in white—and embroider it yourself with your prayer of thanks, or stuff a small pillowslip with herbs, embroider a heart or other emblem (or appliqué one if you prefer) onto it, and secure the open end with a tie made up of all the colored ribbons. It will still be powerful if you do it with care and passion.

THE SPELL PROPER

Make a circle in your main living area with the leaves (or pictures), and the candles tied or encircled with each of the matching ribbons. Sit in the center with your pillow, and the little album or book into which you have placed your photos of the people in your dreams—happy dreams primarily, but those who give you bad dreams too, for these problems should now be released and resolved.

Light the candles and address each color for a moment: look at the red and remember your energy in beginning your tasks; look to the pinky-gold and remember your visions, thinking through what you envisioned your dreams to be; concentrate now on the amber or cherry-pink color, and contemplate your hopes in love; turn your attention to the indigo/blue color, and think about your work duties and aspirations; and so through all the colors, dwelling on the concerns of each color and the chapters that have gone before, as they affect your life, until you come to the golden candle for this chapter and consider the completion—or the thanks—for which you are making an offering.

Once you have collected all of these (color-coded!) thoughts, bow your head, make your prayer of thanks or final hopes, stroke the album containing those who people your world, and ask for many blessings, and wisdom, and a successful conclusion to your affairs. Let the candles burn down a little: do not hurry this.

After a while, blow out each flame and bow once more. Your tasks are complete.

If you have just a small "thanks" to make, or a very simple wish to nudge the spirits a little to end your affairs according to your hopes, simply embrace and inhale your love pillow, and sleep upon your dreams.

CONCLUSION: THIS BRINGS US TO YOUR ULTIMATE LESSON. Your odyssey will have sparked many ideas of your own, and you will have your own signature sense of what it means to be a "witch."

You will have discovered your own ways of working magic, and you should have found the methods that work best for you personally. If you have woven your dreams and magic wisely and well across the year, you will have strengthened your awareness of the world around you, taken charge of many matters in your life, and added fairy dust to the lives of many friends and loved ones—even some who may think you a little strange! THAT'S MAGIC! *Blessed Be.*

)

APPENDIX: **HOW TO DESIGN YOUR OWN SPELL.** The book is arranged so as to make it possible for you to make up your own spell to suit your exact situation; many elements are interchangeable, and once you know what they stand for, you should be able to bring together the ideas and symbols relevant for you. Below is an example of how you could proceed to mix and match for your own perfect spell . . . .

1. DECIDE WHAT IS THE CENTRAL CONCERN OF YOUR SPELL. If it concerns work, for example, is the issue about advancement, or perhaps harassment? Perhaps it's about carving out a career that leads ultimately to financial security? Or is it a spell for love? Are you trying to get an admirer to move faster? Or do you want to reverse an argument? Select the central concern and work around that, consulting the appropriate chapter for the main "recipe" for your spell.

2. ARE THERE OTHER ISSUES INVOLVED? The examples above illustrate that several elements could be part of the problem, so consider the two or three other aspects of your own particular case and add in some symbols and colors from those chapters.

3. WHAT TIME OF THE YEAR IS IT? It may be July, and you need to honor the holly tree in your spell; but if the subject is governed by the rowan moon, you need some materials concerned with that tree as well. Add in any emblem from the rowan chapter, and perhaps the colors associated with this.

So, here is a sample of arranging the elements of a spell.

THE PROBLEM
Let's say you recently broke up with someone, but you've spent some time talking to somebody you've noticed before(!) at an office Christmas party, and you think (hope?) there's an attraction on both sides. With your confidence still a little shaken, you want the other party to initiate things.

THE SOLUTION
1. The subject is love, so look to chapter 3. You will find that the second variation on page 49 fits the main situation very well, but perhaps you'd like to put the past behind you as well as starting something new. Reading the first variation, the symbol of healing yourself with the photo and rose would also apply. You must now try to marry these ideas harmoniously.

2. Your main spell is the Master Love spell in chapter 3. You are asked to select three ribbons and candles, one cherry-pink (for love) and the others to suit. Flame-red is the color of initiating anything (see chapter 1); green is for healing (including healing yourself, see chapter 11); and there's that work connection also (color blue, see chapter 4). Your own favorite color might be purple—which you were also wearing when you met. Pink is the required color, but

choose the other two as you please and as you feel appropriate. You will also need a red ribbon to concentrate on the person beforehand.

3. Consulting the main spell, you find red wine is required, but you are allergic to this; choose white, or, if you don't drink, something nonalcoholic. Also, you are asked to choose an essential oil or some incense to focus your thoughts: but maybe you would rather use the scent the person you like so much was wearing when you met, to make that feeling really immediate again? Fine! Play some music, too, if there was something you can recall playing during the course of that evening. Draw in any elements you want to, and don't worry about too many hard and fast "rules."

4. Treat your photograph as the first variation on page 48 suggests; and lay this to the side as you do your main spell.

You could put an elder twig near your candles for the month you're in (near Christmas), and an ash twig to entreat the blessings of the ash moon which governs the whole subject of love—as in chapter 3.

5. When you have finished working your spell, let it end as you wish it to. Don't worry about how long it takes to burn candles down: when you feel you've done enough, release the magic into the stratosphere! It is always important to release your magic at the end: if you hold onto a spell too tightly, it's like writing a letter that you then don't mail! Your spell must leave you.

So now, think through your situation; decide what is most significant, and blend the ideas, colors, scents, emblems, that appeal to you, and work for your imagination. And that's all there is to it. (But remember not to hurt anyone!) GOOD LUCK.

THE CELTIC MOON CALENDAR

In tune with the idea that the year, and we as individuals, are fluid and growing, this calendar reflects the elastic essence of life and magic working. Use it to work with the natural rhythms of the world, for me it symbolizes the philosophy I have tried to communicate: that nothing is tied down or writ in stone; least of all, time! The months are measured from the full moon, when the moon is at the height of its power. Here are the dates for the full moons, and thus the commencement of each month, for the next three years:

●	BIRCH	ROWAN	ASH	ALDER	WILLOW	HAWTHORN	OAK	HOLLY	HAZEL	VINE	IVY	REED	ELDER
2000	–	JAN. 22ND	FEB. 20TH	MAR. 21ST	APRIL 18TH	MAY 18TH	JUNE 17TH	JULY 16TH	AUG. 15TH	SEPT. 13TH	OCT. 13TH	NOV. 11TH	DEC. 11TH
2001	JAN. 9TH	FEB. 8TH	MAR. 9TH	APRIL 8TH	MAY 7TH	JUNE 6TH	JULY 5TH	AUG. 4TH	SEPT. 2ND	OCT. 2ND	NOV. 1ST	NOV. 30TH	DEC. 30TH
2002	JAN. 28TH	FEB. 27TH	MAR. 28TH	APRIL 27TH	MAY 26TH	JUNE 24TH	JULY 23RD	AUG. 22ND	SEPT. 21ST	OCT. 21ST	NOV. 19TH	DEC. 19TH	–
2003	–	–	–	–	–	–	–	–	–	–	–	–	JAN. 14TH

RELIGION IN WICCA

Wicca is not only about spell-making; in fact it is principally a way of life—and a very religious way at that. Spells are, in a sense, a form of prayer; and it is true that you will derive more from the subject if you understand this religious dimension. You will have seen that many of the spells loosely invite the petitioning of one or other of the ancient gods or goddesses (or a spirit entity), where others aren't demanding on this score. In fact, all systems of ancient magic worked in hand with the power of the gods.

In this book the religious element is very much a matter of choice, and it is written so that it can dovetail with any personal religious feeling. It may help, however, to relate your spell workings back to the magic of the ancients, so here follows a concise list of the most commonly petitioned gods and goddesses in matters related to love. It is worth remembering that the Romans borrowed from the pantheon of Greek gods, adding them in alongside their own—which they seem to have done as the spread of the Roman Empire brought Roman gods face to face with Gallic, Celtic, Teutonic gods, and so on. The ancient Britons trusted their magic to the celebrated Druids (the holy and wise men of the Celts, and it was not unusual for them to omit naming the gods directly in their ceremonies or in swearing oaths. You may choose to do this also.

LOVE: APHRODITE, VENUS (AND CUPID)

The famed and beautiful goddess of love, Aphrodite was the lady to ask for divine intervention in matters of the heart. She had power over seductions, lust, marriage, and flirtation. She was not above playing tricks on mortals and could direct affairs most unsuitably when in the spirit to do so; but if lovers with a genuine heart asked her help and paid her honour, she was ever ready to perform the deed and bring two hearts together.

In this she was ably assisted by her son, Eros, who had a bow and arrow of his own which would strike love into the heart of any his arrow found. In Roman mythology she was called Venus—born, like Aphrodite, from the sea foam and borne to the shore on a shell where the Horae of Spring and Summer waited for her. According to legend, roses appeared at this time, and they have been her flower ever since. Her ally, the cherubic Cupid, is mentioned several times in the book, and is familiarly spoken to on Valentine's Day. The best day for an audience with either is Friday. The angel associated with Venus is Anael.

DIVINATION AND PROPHECY: APOLLO

God of the light, and known in Rome by the same name, Apollo was vested with many powers, but none so significant as that of the oracle. To him one turned to know the signs of the future, including matters of love in the future; and his shrines were many, though none so well known as that in Delphi. He shared with Helios (the actual Solar deity) the power of bringing forth crops as well; and his companions, the Muses, remind us that he was credited as god of the song and the lyre, thus entertainment is shared under his province with Zeus/Jupiter. His day is that of the Sun, Sunday. His flower is the sunflower or marigold. The Archangel Michael is associated with Apollo and the Sun.

OUR DEEP EMOTIONS AND SECRET SELF:
THE MOON: SELENE, LUNA

Companion of the sleeping soul, Selene was the sister of Helios and illuminated the shadowy night with her gold crown. She bathed each night in the ocean and then rose on a steed to watch mortals during the night. It was her love for Endymion, who was granted immortality by Zeus as long as he slept eternally, that brought the faithful rays of the moon each night to caress the sleep of lovers. Her day is Monday, and her flowers are

costmary, white roses (wild), and white poppies. She can be
compared closely with Epona, moon goddess and protector
of horses to the Celts. The Archangel Gabriel is connected with
the Moon.

Marriage, Maternity, and Childbirth: Hera, Juno, Wife of Zeus

Hera was in a sense the deity who presided over all feminine
existence. She shared duties with Aphrodite in presiding over
marriage, but her most important role was as Goddess mother.
Her sacred bird was the peacock, whose feathers resembled the
starry sky. Juno to the Romans (although the Roman Vesta
also presided over fertility and motherhood, as did Maia, who
was even more ancient in origin) she has her parallel in all
cultures as a Mother, notably in Celtic (especially Irish) mythology
to whom she is Brigit (later, St. Brigid); she was Rhiannon
(a true fertility goddess) to the Welsh.

Work with this information as you feel you should; choose
what's right in your heart, and don't in any way be false to what
you believe. Do, however, work wisely and warmly.

INDEX

AUTHORS'
ACKNOWLEDGMENTS

Heartfelt thanks for this beautiful
volume to Luke at johnson banks,
in tandem with the amazing
Sara Morris and her assistant Colin
Campbell. At Quadrille, thanks be
to all – but by name, Kate, Jo Harris
and Jo Barnes, Alice, Peta, and
Camilla: you all work with speed and
grace and wonderful imagination!
And Anne, Alison, Mary, and Marlis:
THANK YOU! Also many thanks to
Lisa and Kate Milton, to Stewart
and all at Jerry's, to Paul Ross,
Caron Keating, and Julia Carling,
who are wonderful to work with;
Guy and Collette at THIS MORNING,
and absolutely everyone at The Old
School Building in Manchester.
My family live with very little of me
through much of the year – thanks
for your patience Zephy and Mantha!
Big hugs to Janet Opie and Joan
Bridgman at the Open University,
who give lots of time. Rory Higham:
thanks for road-testing all my books!
Thanks also Orlando and Lily for
kind words! Lastly, but never least,
thanks, hugs, and warm witchy wishes
to B*Witched – Edele, Keavy, Sinead,
and Lindsay – the loveliest fairy
god-daughters anyone could ask for!
Keep up the enchanting stuff, girls!
BLESSED BE. xxx